13/9/95

IMAGINE INVENTING YELLOW

IMAGINE INVENTING
YELLOW

New and Selected Poems of

M. C. RICHARDS

Station Hill

Published by Station Hill Literary Editions, under the Institute for Publishing Arts, Inc., Barrytown, New York 12507. Station Hill Literary Editions is supported in part by grants from the National Endowment for the Arts, a Federal Agency in Washington, D.C., and by the New York State Council on the Arts. Special appreciation to Dillane Schloth, Dede Levering, and Donna Horie for their contributions to this project.

Back cover photo of the author by Gerry Williams.

Text and cover design by Susan Quasha.

Type by Delmas Typesetting.

Distributed by the Talman Company, 150 Fifth Avenue, New York, New York 10001.

Library of Congress Cataloging-in-Publication Data

Richards, Mary Caroline.
  Imagine inventing yellow / M.C. Richards.
    p.   cm.
  ISBN 0-88268-127-3 (paper); ISBN 0-88268-102-8 (cloth):
  I. Title
PS3568.I3156I44   1991
811'.54—dc   91-48976
                                                                 CIP

Manufactured in the United States of America.

Contents

Poems from Poems (1947)

Poems from Centering (1964, 1989)

Poems from The Crossing Point (1973)

List of Illustrations

Paintings by Thomas S. Buechner, Sr.

to Lily Kate, my mother,
who pinned poems to the kitchen curtains

Freeing the Imagination

RHUBARB architecture:

pillars and parasols polychrome,
cantilevered,
more slopes than right angles . . .

    a gathering . . .
        tent city, this rhubarb patch:
        pink struts, green canvases,
        darkened roofing of deep fiber —

If it is to be eaten,
        is it not a sacrament?

Shall we bless this
        sculptured meal — this
        edible community?

CARROT:

a flurry of foliage spun to green filigree and
a golden root deep, like a dagger —
a row of molten daggers,
of orange flames taught by winds
        to sharpen, to lengthen.
A figure of eight left to dream above ground,
the fire's bright burrowing into lemniscate below.

        Feel the strong swing!

Preface

"Imagine Inventing Yellow" is a tribute to the forsythia bush! Yes, actually the sudden yellowing of landscape that happens in early spring, when golden Forsythia emerges from Her winter twigs, this takes our breath away. This does it. Imagine inventing yellow! How does shining sun color come to be the coat of this shaggy bush? Whoever could first imagine the color of flowers? Who but Herself? Or the curve of a cherry, indenting like a heart to receive its stem....

The colors come from the spirit of Natura, the Goddess who inspires the forming and coloring. Natura is the birthing pool of nature; she is the living Being of the forces that generate, that are born into sense perception, that grow. Colors are a bridge from here to Her—from the blossom to its source beyond the senses. The matrix, i.e. the mother of the senses, is supersensible. Our sense perception opens like fingers at the end of a long arm reaching from the realm of Natura. We can feel this birth into sense perception when we look at a bud forming and swelling and beginning to open. It moves fast. Where does it come from? It does not travel up the stalk or out the twig! It comes out of a different kind of space—an "etheric" space. The bud is called into being by warmth and light, and develops not by adding substance, but by unfolding from within itself. It comes from within, out of a spaceless space, the other side of matter. Mathematicians have called this "gegen-raum" or "negative space."

Another example of this birthing process, out of an inner space that comes before the sense perception, is our experience of speaking. Where is the word, where are the words before we speak them? Do they lie curled in our larynx like seeds, like thoughts? We are in a natural and spontaneous conversation. We have not rehearsed what we will say to one another. And yet, the words come. Obviously they come from some non-verbal realm, transforming into sound with lightning speed. What depths one has as a sensual being! Into these depths Imagination looks and brings us pictures of a cosmic layering: one small bird sings from source and the ripples of its song heal us, make us whole, reconnect us with source.

When I am painting, I have sometimes this extraordinary experience. My ordinary consciousness transforms into a participation in the colors themselves. I live in the gestures of the brush, my arm moving, the colors streaming and overlapping and separating and flooding the plane with their light and dark. I am so moved by the transcendence of this Color Experience—so delivered over into another realm that is real and not made up—that I am sometimes overcome with awe and appreciation. What is this awe but prayer and thanksgiving? It is to this condition that our meditations may aspire: to bring us to the Door, to the Crossing Point, where we may stand in the full dimension of reality: outer and inner, yellow and the Being of Yellow.

The poetry of this book stands in this Door. The poem happens when the Being of Yellow touches the flesh of the flower, and the Forsythia blooms. The supersensible archetype touches personal experience, and poetic excitement ignites. It is always more than personal, and yet grounded in the personal. It takes both sides of the Door to give the full swing of human truth.

Imagine Inventing Yellow is a book of poems celebrating "what imagination means."

> Across the Golden Gate from San Francisco
> Between the bay and the Pacific
> Lies Marin County.
>   When I was living
> In Berkeley I would sometimes spend Sunday
> Walking across the ridge above Muir Woods
> Between Mill Valley and Stinson Beach.
>   Once
> I walked washed there in empty air and heard
> Between the ocean's grand oblivion and
> The white stair of the city one small bird
> Sing, all prodigal, to his bare theater.
>   Since,
> He inhabits my mind high on a wire and
> Wonders me what imagination means.

Imagination means singing to a wide invisible audience. It means receptivity to the creative unconscious, the macrocosmic mind, artistic mind. It makes erotic philosophers of us, as we imagine the world in images that make whole. To imagine is to give birth to—to embody the spirit in word and picture and behavior. The world will change when we can imagine it differently and, like artists, do the work of creating new social forms.

BEHOLDING is also a way of imagining, and when heart and throat open, song arises—as simple as breathing. Behold, as spring comes, "a god falling into life!"

Poetry of the senses connects and reconnects the body, soul, and spirit. "Pelted by beauty" in an Indian flower ritual, we activate

> "a cellular reordering, each tiny vessel
> lovecrazed, opening.
> ... Now truly are we god's fools,

lilies of the field, no thought for the morrow,
feeding strangers, and comforting the fearful ..."

In "A Westerner Visits Australia" the poet asks, "How shall we love / before we have lost everything?" Here is the imaginative faculty of "seeing through" into the unnamable deep within every name, so that even a one-liner resonates with what is not said: "A black swan has a red mouth." An alchemy of eros.

Imagining is participating in. It is a crucial transformation from Spectator Thinking to Creative Becoming. And there are signs that this transformation is under way. Spectator Thinking is able to document, to record, to analyze, to deduce. It has a kind of statistical objectivity and, as such, has been the basic discipline of higher education, turning out engineers, scientists, economists, computer specialists. This kind of thinking is not good at understanding what is really going on or at implementing creative alternatives. Its quality is mechanical rather than organic. It was developed as the appropriate coordinate of a mechanistic model of the universe—a phenomenon like a big machine, operating by mechanical laws. Results of this conception are the pollution and destruction of earth. Failure to have a holistic picture of the world, to comprehend how toxic the invisible world has become ... (it is what we cannot see that is poisoning us) ... ah, this failure is stimulating a rediscovery of life sources. And in part this rediscovery is enabled by a thinking that participates in the formative forces of continuing creation. This is imaginative thinking, with a strong element of empathy within it. Empathy tends toward compassion, a "feeling with." Here, "feeling" is a way of knowing, more than an emotion. We know by the "feel" of a thing. We may have a "feeling" for wholeness before any formulation of it. Actually, we may not need the formulation.

The development of an organic thinking, i.e. a thinking that unfolds in the stages of actual living process, may be fostered by a meditative observing of Natura. Just to follow the metamorphosis of the leaves on a buttercup, for example, takes one through a formative sequence up the stalk that has nothing to do with logic. It has to do with the way formative energy works, how differentiation and rhythms occur, how, for example, leaves may become smaller as they develop further—and the surprising leap into colored petals and erect stamens. The plant grows in opposite directions simultaneously, from the beginning when the seed germinates and the root digs down into the dark earth and the seedling leaves open up and out into light and air. This principle, of inherent paradox, can be understood through the geometry of the lemniscate or moebius strip. It is of inestimable value in understanding the formative paradoxes in one's human nature: deeply rooted and freely imagining! Heavily gravity endowed and enlightened through listening with the inner ear. We are clay and we are word.

I live at the present time in a working community, based on biodynamic agriculture and gardening, following suggestions made by Rudolf Steiner early in this century for the healing of the life forces of the earth. We offer a training program for agricultural apprentices, and in it I offer a course I call "The Renewal of Art through Agriculture." It is my purpose in this course to help the students (the farmers and gardeners) lift their perceptions into their Imagination, where perceptions may be enriched by a "spiritual feel" and reconnected to Source. I receive some indication from these individuals that indeed there is a longing for this realm of universal feeling and for the freedom to imagine what they are experiencing. All week they work with hoes and tractors (so to speak), and then they come to the studio and we work with clay and color and the sounds and meanings of words. Recently we ended a term by making masks: not to conceal, but to reveal the Being of Natura in some one of her epiphanies, happy or wounded. The masks were to be held before our faces and spoken through. What would these Beings say? They were nodes on the lifeline of the great tree of life. They spoke of connection and disconnection—of ecstatic union and griefstricken destruction. The masks were the countenances of Natura's living aspects. Being thus ensourced, art is renewed. And along with the art, the artistperson. We were renewed: deepened, made more reflective, made more acute in our listening to one another, more astounded in our beholding, simpler in our stories as we heard their divine genesis.

At the end of the session, the students lingered, stayed. They didn't want to leave the world of imagination that they had helped to create and that felt so alive and juicy and touching. They know they cannot live without it. The earth is dying because we have not been able to cross over into the double realm. We have been doing the tasks of materialism, cut off from spirit. Now the bonds are loosening. An evolutionary step is being taken. We are re-entering, rediscovering, renewing, recreating, open to a transformation of our thinking, of our way of conceiving the world. Imagination is opening us with pictures and images. Inspiration is responding to our revitalized listening. Intuition receives us into a union and interdependence, a wholeness.

The child in us tends to know these things already. Perhaps that is why she tends to be so abused in our culture. The child is witness to another realm that challenges our will to control and to dominate. Often in ourselves there is this severe conflict betwen our mystical child and the materialistically educated adult we have become. Between the mystical and the secular souls in our breasts. Part of what one hopes to do with one's poetry and one's life is to awaken Imagination as a light that can shine within all one's behavior and experience. To bring the mystical awe into the secular cynicism and despair. To lift the hoe and the tractor into wands and divine engines! To live in the real world!

Remember the cautionary story of the zen sage who said, "Now that I'm enlightened, I'm just as miserable as ever!" Suffering is not eliminated by Imagination. It is beheld in its colors and in its meaning.

The poems in this book span more than 40 years. The title comes from one that appeared in my first published *POEMS*, handset and printed by myself at Black Mountain College in 1947. "What Imagination Means" is also from that first book.

Beheld through Imagination, all things are lit from within. All experience carries the mystery of source and yields both poetry and truth. This insight has become my poetics.

It has developed slowly and steadily, growing into a kind of writing that softens the categories, intent as it is upon source. More and more my work has found its way into expression that is hard to define. This journey of "freeing the Imagination" can be shared in my books: *Centering, The Crossing Point, Toward Wholeness: Rudolf Steiner Education in America, The Public School and the Education of the Whole Person*. Poems from these books have been selected for this collection.

This poetics is boldly expressed in "Nine Easter Letters on the Art of Education," the title chapter of *The Crossing Point*.

The piece is composed for the space of the page as well as in the two colors of my typewriter ribbon, red and black. In the headnote I describe the impulse behind the work. "I also wanted to assimilate into the flow of the talk the different moods of 'voice,' rather than limiting myself to the monochrome delivery of lecture models. I moved therefore as naturally as I could through a continuity of poetry and story and exposition to the closing prayer and sung song. This was the first time that I had made a song to sing as part of a lecture. This one seems to me to have in its form the flavor of a 'spiritual.' Also for this occasion I wanted to connect the talk with the Easter season in which it occurred."

Another chapter, based on my work at the Curriculum Lab, Goldsmiths College, University of London, concludes with a summary that turns inevitably into the rhythms and emotions of verse. I sing to my English colleagues and co-workers. I hear the song as I type, moved to commitment beyond thought. In a simple litany, I list the names of the roses the members brought from their gardens each morning. Artistic mind births the days and the behavior. Poetry is its natural expression.

> Transcending the grammars we teach and learn,
> can we own up to who we are
>   and the mystery?
> Can we awaken

xv

ourselves in ourselves,
     and in ourselves
each other?

"Wrestling with the Daimonic" is also conceived and composed in the crossing point where categories dissolve, or rather, where they have not yet congealed. It lives in the speaking voice. Bouts with the Daimonic! They are imaginative and musical. And they move poetic art further into the open field where it means to live.

In the last dozen years I have found myself framing a so-called prose piece with poems. I would finish writing something sensible and well-argued and find myself dissatisfied, as if it were incomplete. And so I would then be inspired to write, for example, the Angel Poems, to begin and end the piece. Or "Anthem" and "Hymn," which frame the booklet on The Public School. These pieces set the stage in the Imagination from which the prose can speak and be heard in a certain coloring. A certain mood. We need to allow the divine to irradiate the secular, the artistic to irradiate the intellectual. We need to welcome artistic mind, holistic mind, cosmic mind. We need to let intellect drop away like dry leaves as Imagination and Empathy emerge from the meristem. Imagination beholds from a divine-and-earthly source. It reveals. It does not manipulate or seek to persuade. Clarity? You want clarity? Look through here!

There are two small "portfolios" of poems in this collection: "Six Christmas Poems" (which were also privately printed in 1989) and "Poems for Paintings by Thomas S. Buechner, Sr." The painter and I were colleagues at Haystack Mountain School of Crafts in Maine. In 1986, during a shared summer session, he gave me a catalogue of his recent show. I was deeply astonished and moved by the beauty and depth of some of his paintings, though certainly his work is very different from my own. And in the autumn, upon receiving a print of "White Daffodil," I was precipitated into a poetry that seemed astonishing and moving in its own turn ... as if the archetype of Still-life, Landscape, and Portrait had given its palette to language. And so these poems began:

The painter unfolds his easel
and the shadows change color.

In the weeks, months, years that followed, others were written, some of which are included here. Thomas Buechner's paintings hang in the National Museum of American Art, the Metropolitan Museum of Art, Alice Tully Hall, and many collections.

The most recent poem in this selection is "A Westerner Visits Australia," written in January, 1990, in Tasmania, on a journey "down under." On the flight across the Pacific, I had been reading in *Pagan Meditations* the one on Aphrodite. She was active in my imagination during my stay, and it is she who steps out of the sea to begin the poem. I could not have been more surprised when the last six lines wrote themselves, and "Easter" suddenly was announced. The poem had been moving along at quite a pace, into the waters of Captains Bligh and Cook, into the rainforest of Bruny Island, sailing the waters of Venus/Aphrodite. Then a sudden halt! We make camp. We make landfall. And the next day is EASTER, when the western ego and Aphrodite merge and surrender to Love transformed and released. They bring the gift of their tears to the divine feet of Love. These feet are sacred as well to the aboriginals. The journey "down under" is completed, having begun at the sacred red mother rock, Uluru. A new way has opened into the tenderness of the final lines.

> There is a camp here in the maelstrom,
> and tomorrow landfall,
> and the next day EASTER,
> when we-Aphrodite, a radiant vortex,
> wet with our tears the feet of love
> and dry them with our hair.

In imagination we see the figures of the archetypes as they emerge, and sense their footsteps as they pass by, numinous.

POSTSCRIPT

In the introduction to the 1989 anniversary edition of *Centering,* I said that the big change I would make if I were to rewrite that book would be to dethrone the masculine pronoun: the "he" who rules the grammar of our language. I would add also a concern for the use of the generic "man" when one is talking about the transgender human being. I am familiar with the arguments for leniency here, how "man" really means "mankind" which means everybody, but actually everybody is not "man." And just now in our human consciousness we are becoming so much more sensitive to the implications of what we say out of habit, out of male-dominated schooling and philosophy and theology, out of unconscious collusion. Certainly it has taken me my whole adult life to acknowledge how my adoration of the male has sown grief. God knows there is nothing wrong with falling in love, but there is something awful that happens when the beloved's feeling changes, and one's world falls to ashes. One has not been taught that love and freedom are angelic beings in a subtle sacred relationship, not to be quickly translated as either obsession or permissiveness. The terror of loss is the terror of loss of self. The healing may engender an individuation process, devoutly to be wished. It is not the love that suffers, but the desire. When I am no longer desired by the male of my choice, I die—I am diminished—I reject myself—I am swallowed up in hopelessness and despair. Why? Because, the story goes, the love of the male empowers my life as a woman.

Perhaps it needed to be so at one time historically. It does not need to be so now. As the true self awakens, compassionate love awakens. Some of my poems celebrate romantic love, its glories and its tragedies, in authentic experience. But there is one long poem, the last chapter of *Centering*, in which the unconscious masculine preference of our language is no longer tolerable to me. "Recovery of the Child in Manhood" was so titled out of a play on the title of Cecil Harwood's book on Steiner education *Recovery of the Child in Adulthood*. I apparently thought it was time to turn the tables and right the imaginative balance. The issue now is the use of "Man" and "Manhood" to carry the spiritual content of the human being.

I have decided to go beyond acknowledging the sexism of the language. For this book, I have changed the language. In most instances, I think the poem gains. In some, most notably perhaps in the title, it loses music but gains clarity: "Recovery of the Child in Adulthood."

The original version is still to be found in *Centering*. It has been said that certain forms may work well for us, but when they cease to work, they become immediately toxic. Truths change. So be it.

The three most recent poems in this volume are "A Westerner Visits Australia," "Deep Ecology," and "The Shaman Comes Home." I sense in them a deep sea change reflected in my own psyche: the integration of the female in the Embracing Orbit of Love.

New Poems

1980 - 1990

Poet

I put on my poet's shirt
and birds fly through.
Birds perch in me and
their throats tremble.
Their high singing builds
in me a listening love.

Clothes are the sheaths
of my being — so many old dreams of
changing dress, unable to decide,
always late for the occasion,
what to wear?

    Now the dreamer is at rest:
she wears the nests, the eaves
and orchards. Wears the tall pine
of the white-throated sparrow
in the city walk-up — the gutters
and sills — understanding a language
she does not know, hearing the inaudible.

Potter

This flat plate. This ladle and bowl.
Clay whirled on a wheel, raised slowly to the table.
Straight and curved, our primal gestures
take and give — speak out about
the way we stand and breathe.
Every leaf is saucer for the bread.
Every falling drop prepares its cup.
Always we are eating and drinking earth's body,
Making her dishes.
     Potters like sun and stars
     perform their art —
     endowed with myth,
     they make the meal holy.

Angel Poems

I: Introit - Opening Song

In this valley of mountains,
this ocean of deserts,
we gather. We put our ears to the ground
and listen for steps. We put our eyes to the glass
and look for visions. We put our hands to the
clay and touch a swelling breast.
Far out to sea someone sails.
We gather into an ear, a glance, an embrace
to receive our angels. Around us they hover,
plaiting their feathers, gazing into the crystal
of the inner eye, holding the neck of a wild swan.
Ha! Hear their rustle, they are ready to speak.
They tell us to press on with our questions — to
rethread our needles, wedge our clay and prepare our canvas.
They tell us their crystal is ground in our devotion.
The swan carries them through our clay spheres,
their braids are the layers of our colors.
Our worlds are one, they say. Look! They are all about us! ...
weaving and dancing, afire with high heat, pale and
pearl-like, silvery, and carved like hard wood. What
are they singing? "In art is a communion of worlds!"

II: Benediction

A flutter of feathers, a song, a
stir of air — "Keep the faith,"
they sing: "human dreams are angel food,
human deeds are angel drink.
When you gather together like this,
imagination deepens across the heavens,
and we see your souls trafficking between the worlds.
Through the crossing point pours a living fountain;
your art will guide you to its waters.
Farewell. We are with you always. Feel
in your inner eye our iris crystal
and under your feet the web of the swan."

To My New Goat

O THOU
O COW
   nanny, nanette,
   thy udder's awry, thy
   crown's awag, thy tail a-
   toss.
      ma-a-a-a-a, bleat,
   blat, blut, blot. Thy shiny turds
   a-toddle. Whos'ever got thee by thy teat,
   hot, has thee, has thee not.
      I love your square black eyne, your
   leafy ear, your mask of teeth, your
   trot.
      Anahid, beloved goddess,
   give me to drink. To suck.

For John Cage on his 75th birthday

Dear John Cage
It is already dusk
and the cows are not yet in —
already dawn, are not yet out. Listen.
It sounds ever thus, the breathing.
40 years ago
you touched down at our landing,
young planets,
inwardly orbiting.   tirra lirra loo
Our first words were a courtship!
tirra lirra   day in and day out
Shall I tell you the secret of our mystery?
You are a preacher and I am a missionary.
We make love for justice
and delight: kindliness, laughter, and rage.
Macrobiotic eros, you nourish the ends of the earth
in ever new beginnings.
The cows, John, the cows are banging their udders like soft cymbals,
and the milkers are playing the teats like bell ropes
tugging and letting go. The music, my God, the music!

Music

"Musical experience is something which concerns the whole of the human being, and the ear has here a function that is quite different from the one usually ascribed to it.... The ear is really there for the purpose of overcoming the resounding of the tone in the air and reflecting back into our inner being the pure etheric experience of tone."

(Rudolf Steiner, "The Human Being's Experience of Tone."
Art in the Light of Mystery Wisdom, p. 116)

Just as I suspected!
All that sound is not the music at all!
The music is really inaudible!

The ear, he said, is a threshold:
    sipped through bone, the nectar of tone.
Ah, that's the rapture of listening:
    intimacy closer than senses!
Tone, we become one another.
Essential angel, you make love the meaning.

Music of the spheres then
is this hearing, — this union?
O, always I have known music and love
are more than meet the ears,
known the Wellspring sings to an inner hearing,
deep in the body of gods.

How to Rake Water

Dry Water

The pull of tines through sand rakes water into waves.

Dry water pools into dust.

Take the stream of time and rake it into hours. Let
the dry flowing future slake the earth's thirst.

Water wings whip the great shapes of flying and rake
the buoyant water into circles.

I am this water and this rake — combing my ocean
into piles of stone.

Water

SPREAD THIN TURNS INTO RAIN
HOLDS WITHIN BANKS THE CUP OF SEAS
RUNS DOWN THE MOUNTAIN'S CHIN AND FOAMS IN THE
    GREENBEARD OF TREES
STREAMS THROUGH MY BODY AGAINST GRAVITY LIKE SAP
SLAPS AND DODGES REBUTTAL, THE OSCILLATION OF TIDES
COLD, CONNECTS ME WITH THE MELTING GLACIER,
    DISSOLVES ALL DIFFERENCES
FINDS ITS LEVEL, TAKES THE EASIEST WAY, LIKE A SAGE
PLAYING, THE DANCING SPRAY DECLARES ITS FREEDOM
FILLED WITH IT, I DIE INTO DREAMS WALKING ON WATER

Wave

The landscape lies before me in a great wave—high where I
stand, then sloping into the valley where the sheep graze
and higher again in the distance. The rhythm of sunrise
moves the light also in a subtle undulation from beyond
the distant hills into the pasture bottomland and, ever
lightening, washes swiftly up the grassy slope.

I stretch out on the ground and, like a body surfer, feel
the wave move under me; ever pulsing, the hours are lost
in rhythm.

A wave moves through water like enchantment through an
evening walk.

The wave moves through water, changing its shape.
The water moves through the wave, and the wave is still.

Letter: March 29

The bright wig wags,
the hairy noodle wobbles,
jays wangle foot-room, I'm telling you, it makes
eye-balls jittery. Can't believe my eyes half—
looks like the apple orchards are being roasted
in rusty auras, they flinch not but stand
corrective. Daily, brush along the road
grows Spanish with fever, peppery red,
diagramming blood systems in thin air.

Spatulas of wind toss paper like flapjacks,
icky mist evaporating snow
shovelsfull of bucking backbreaking pewter-colored rocks
revealed. They've been there all the time, who'd have known it, these
past storms.

Mouse-down, it must be, pink
and flaky, now flies, rosecoloring my glasses.
Tenderest babes in the world, mice.
New-born spring, like old times, what am I
saying. Old-born spring, like new times?

Wasps are crawling around in my living room,
half-baked, blind and trying to get going I guess.
Spooned one outdoors today, poor dumb sap,
lucky I was the one.

But to get back about those seeds,
there's dynamite in those capsules,
dynamite. Death and dynasties go together?
Our old selves, about to sprout? Where have we been, all winter?
Ever? Is it like space, a round track
where we meet ourselves coming back?
Is it like time, the egg we've laid
coming to meet us well-hatched? I don't think there are any trade-ins
here, I think spring is straight.

It's like a big hearth somebody's blowing on and the light begins to poke
and meander and breathe

with somebody's breath, and that funny radiance
you might say luminosity, like light was not only in the filament
but outside the bulb too, like nature stands in it,
poplars in green, willows in gold, parsley in yellow,
hellebore in lime, maples in aubergine, lichens in ash,
and grass blades like rays of sun yellow and sharpdarting
out of that big bag in the earth where last summer's sun
was stored.

It's enough to make your heart beat as loud as the surf
we seem to be lounging and plunging in. Skin-divers
of the upper air, will you go along with me?
Bright fantastic fish? Mouths always going?
Rapture of the vasty depths? Rivers like layers of skin
peeling up through the atmosphere? Plenty of sound?
Water, they say, is an especially great conductor.
Shall we let ourselves be led?

Walking through fields here is walking through crossfire!
birds bursting in air, red shreds,
earth's balloon spongy under foot, breaking,
I see holes in it, hear the air escaping
followed by troops. Talk about oceans! Talk about
tight-wires! You can't walk steady around here, it's
positively on film, the cameras are all in motion,
knocked on their uppers by some bud-thrust.
Those bud-thrusts, you could have seen them yourself
last week, big stubby green snoots slooping up out of the mud
in last year's whiskers, where's the rest of the body, what's behind
that big push.

My nerves are wet and misty,
juiced.
The great being is astir, that's all you can say,
let the oracle speak, its limbs are working.

Summer

The blue of your body is
chicory laden: pink blush
inside a hyacinth hue. I walk
into morning, and the blue smear
in the fields calls out for naming:
ecstatic syllables!
                        Every year
I suffer this enslavement, beseech
the magical tremulous color, to solve
its riddle. Passion groans in chains,
and dreams of a dazzling transfiguration:
all the pigment drained away, and the stalk
prepared for burning.

                        Where will it go,
this summer's epiphany? Where enfolded
will its angel rest? to manifest in the rhythms of time and
the field's mystical glory . . .

Heirs to Persephone and Pluto,
our innocence is rooted in desire.
Passion and sacrifice mix the colors of our season.

A Land

for Jaquetta Hawkes

i

makes humus they say, the fallen glade.
each man, the earth, erodes and fills.

igneous upheavals, and denudations, O

keep us our clay and basalt, our
soft beds and shale,
keep us our deserts and our caves

fossil-wise fancy dreams dig
and my millioned history spins
spins by the sun
spins presently
spins
in the big tent, O
caution! . . . this bush makes flesh,
tell scientists, and this hand makes
stone. Pulsing sea, in my veins' salt,
remember me!

ii

all loves's fine bones, like lacey herring,
keep—
in rock, in our body's rock,
in granite, of the heart,
fine, thin, curved ribs, and treasure pockets of eyes
and the spine's flick
all the imperishable outline
in pen and ink? no, in fact, there, there
in the rock bed, in earth
which is what we have,
in changing dust, which is who we are,
carrying our beloved ghosts in our own bodies (our plot of ground)
our plot of ground, forgetting

and crying out for them; then suddenly
waked
to a skull's weight, a knee we carry
in us—
last in, the geology of, our limbs!

Time, Honored

I

In the waters of time I pasture.

II

Rinse
    in slippy. what kind of bubble
do I swim in, rainbow running?

        immerse: will grab with my fly-feet
            its vaulting skin,
      this I like best: to
          walk it, its give,
    to let it run me, down me, under and

                hugged, by th'ooze of
"I tell all" time (All! Told!); taste in your drench
        the holly flick of your
           tale.
      Between my legs, bosom, and beat,
    the nursling laps. A taste of time,
        in the ear's tick,

      nick-ory nick-ory tock
    the mouse ran up my clock
      he had his fun and down he run
    and after the mouse the clock

              grock

III

Hook
    I hang on, route I
ride, around.

Time, I like best. Choir; a choir lasts
and winds its hands.
      Like a bath.

O-

dalisque, bloomers bloated by, lie looking:
at the pie of time, a shadow eats it. Do you,
sometimes,
passing? Inside, air worn (care (for it) worn) wearing it, I
glide through, pressurized. I
relieve myself, at its urinal.
      In my ears, *hear,* its helmet, of mist.

In drifts, coarsens a passageway.

IV

     's tub
a parasol —
             a mouthful, a piece of bread—
8th Avenue
            th'air lowalong sand
            something up my nose
            gum on my shoes
            juice of a half-open clam:
                       closing.

V

     Adorned, as in an old gown of my mother's,
shaking its fringe as I sleep—
     step, in

     — help myself to,
choke on, hiccup up, swallow at the end of a string:
     :
     Dabbing away the last flecks of foam, I
gladden time's couch
              aplenty . . . on my hands, in

my ears, nails, down the mouth
of my sex I have,

      treasure. I SPEND.
      Is MY LOVE.

VI

    This I like best. to

             be in
        time, to be idle to
             have
        time.
             This I like best.
        to be idle, to be in
        time, to have
        time.
             This I like best.

Autumn Grandeur

Autumn grandeur lives in leaves
from their first budding.
Invisibly the colors layer
beneath the green. When
cold breaks its hold, the old
leaf begins to die, disclosing
as it goes, the red the yellow the bronze
array of dying.
      And so it goes
with us as well: destined
from our first life-filled shouts
to die and the hour, the place,
the final cause layered in our flesh
as in the leaf — and all the brightness
of the life between, the gatherings.
      How wrongly we are taught:
that death is enemy to life, when all our days
are in the palette of the dying green.
Were it not for its loosening hold,
there would be no theater
of color, no pageantry, no turning
leaves.

Moon Poems I-IV

MOON I

The black hill
     like the nose of a seal,
and the moon
     like a bright ball bounced
upward and floating.

We hills are seals at play
     in the night fall.
We moons, nudged by the
     velvety snouts,
roll into a single gleam,
returning the sun's aim.

I will paint these
     veils and volumes,
I will paint the
     bright single face
dreaming of suns.

MOON II

All day the sounds of
chimes and the gentle toning
as from a swaying bell
leaning across the sky.

In the bright sun of darkness,
the moon shines — shines and tones —
a bell kept aloft
by measured beats.

O bell of my heart
through the darkness of day
travelling! O bell
swaying in your arch
from rise to set, and
sounding!

Moon III

Moon mask,
hiding the cold cinder,
the floating boulder of itself.
High through the sky the moon swings.
High below, the earth spins,
a gorgeous rock in the teeth of beasts,
the great circle of star signs.

Look up, wherever you are,
to the masked moon. Let
light droop and show the dark
sorrow. Our nightgod lives
off the sun, like a grape
rubbed free of its bloom and shining.

Now comes the true mask,
golden, and the godface
recreated. It is the engenderer.
It speaks in mountain peaks
and valleys, piles of ash, shadows —
where the moon fares fresh.

Moon IV

O moon, make morning new,
make the night splendid.

O moon, release our days into
another time, unmeasured.

Freely you range the plains;
sculpture and prayer
model you.

Moon feast, moon mouth
undisguised, unwithered,
filled with night taste,
unbroken the night's bread.

Moon, give us wildness too,
make us glad —
take us to the night pool
where you double yourself.

Grasping and clutching itself
                    into a ball,
moon left earth's side, taking
a pride of wishes and wanting,
taking the hard contracted cold.

I stand on earth where the moon
                    was inserted,
feeling its force now working
                    from afar.

O moon you are a dancer stopped
            in your tracks, no,
your movements are lost in growth.

Teach us the slow changes.

Your Name, Florida

Yes and it is just about that way with the ocean too:
the song rippling along, and the sea in stitches nipping and tucking.
And the river yes it is that Indian lagoon, a broad leaf of blue,
a vine narrowing and straying. There is that bird place stuffed,
stuffed with wings, necks, heads, and outcry, and thousands settle in
for the night's dark needs. Oh those elbows of birds,
pouchy gullets, slow-motion legs and necks like a shepherd's crook.
What Egyptian mystery hangs by a feather on this egret here,
and what alchemical rite bleeds in this pelican's breast?
Yes that white ruffle at the horizon line
and the ginger sand, the pine poking itself outward in green fringe,
hibiscus doubleyolk, and yoga palms stretched like flying fish.
Breathing deep, the shore line fills to the clouds, the cliff.
And soul drinks in the gale and the song.
Heliotrope, sunturned, sunturning, sun how you do do it
here yes in this land of swelling air, water, fruit and flowers,
this place of fruitful swelling, yes that's what it means, your name, *Florida.*

Behold

Behold Behold
in the eyes of the sea the spell is spoken.
Watery creatures we are, living on land.
How full of fire and air, fluid and crystalline.
So formed, our lives are the dreams of the world.

Each coming through the door of self,
we carry rays of light reciprocal.
We gather into one to make a truth,
each shining bit an offering of the sum.

What inner hunger rises toward the Good?
What inner source unfolds the mandala we learn?
Now here like artists in our search
we make a vessel for the spirit's birth.

Behold Behold
the Mystery whose music is our song.
"Weep. Be innocent. Forgive. Press on."
The song sings us. We are its tune.

St. John's Day,
June 24

Sanguine, he said. Out the window
the long gaze to elderflowers
in the midst of grief.
　　　　All June could be the parade,
the cortege leading to St. John's Day,
midsummer's divide. Quick now
the downslope to December.
Now here in June the wildhaired John
spills over their heads the holy Jordan,
baptizing. And 6 months hence
the Christ's epiphany — the last the latest
brow to be wetted. "I decrease
that he may increase," John said.
　　　　So in this month of roses, lives
the story of earth's turnabout, her
blossoming, her fading, her ascending,
in the dark blood of elderberries.

Poem for St. John the Baptist's Deathday, August 29

The larkspur age, a child at seven
or nine — then white daisies braided in
at ten or eleven — exquisitely timed
in midsummer's measure.
The lush temptations of fifteen:
sweet william, bleeding heart, peony—
John's birthday in the desert sun
smoulders toward disaster.
Herodias, iris hot with scent,
waits, breaks at the larynx. Sudden
eclipse, the solstice passes,
midsummer's eve and bonfire.
The countenance of flowers signals
through the flames. John's head falls.

Nirvana, or "The Mothers"
after Goethe's Faust

It's a dark gargle of sound that rumbles
us round its edge, a summery interlace,
and delivers by design to the pool's lip.
O fledgling, look into that sightless place
and see how emptiness is filled full.
Not densities but light, twilit cascade
of sounding signatures, a ripe abyss.
        See how I drop my hook in these waters
and catch sea wind! All nonsense:
this agitation, this expectancy,
soft succulents to feed soul's gluttony!
        Once wedded now to the primal SHE
an altered alphabet of self will be.

The Sea Has Wings

"The sea has wings," she said, pointing
toward the emerald rush and shimmering.

"The sea has wings and downy breast
folded in the shoulders of the shore.

"They are moon wings, Diana's chaste,
buoyant, beating in the space
between," she said.

"The sea has wings enfolded into birds,
unfolding . . . their music marks
the shores of the earth."

Said the sea, "I press my wide flight
into passageways:

                the salmon in a tumult of wings
                leaps the cascade. The surge of the sea
                sends her home to the riverpool.
                Under the fathering wings she spends
                her love, fluttering like petals."

"I have wings," said the sea, "and
they fly in fishes' gills;
my birdcries weave in the waves."

Holy Splinters and Toothpicks

This spring I watched an old man, Thaddeus Peck, make a tree graft. He brought some tiny bits of a pink hawthorn to graft onto a mean-looking wild thorn apple. Those grafts were no bigger than splinters or toothpicks! Teensy little bits of tissue, didn't look like nuthin, but in them a life power, totally invisible to the natural eye but present to the inner eye of imaginative knowledge in Thad's being: able to transform the quality of treeness coming up through that big root — transforming the thorn apple into a pink flower. All I have ever wanted to say about looking at life from the inside, about seeing into inner forms as generating outer forms, about art and science, is present right there in what Thad did. A connection between invisible and visible — and an awareness of the particularity of forms, the importance of where he positioned the grafts — the tools, the hot wax, the saw, the wedge and mallet, and now the waiting for the supersensible power lines in that growth layer to get to flowing. Should grow three to four feet this season if it's a good graft, he said. It will change the whole environment of the garden.

We shall see wood as countenance of invisible sun cycles, miniature nuclear worlds, supersensible dynamics of coming into being and dying away, the tree rings, the actions of fluids and minerals and oxygen molecules and the combustion of growth and decay, the rising sap and falling leaves. How the tree is feeding earth and air, and is fed by. How the tree marries the human hand and the door is born, the archway, the lintel, the threshold, the rafter —Brancusi's King and Queen are born — the table, the altar, the box, the wheel, the cart, the cross. Tree. Tree of life. Holy splinters and toothpicks.

29

Clay Journal

1.

An angelic ocean feeds at the shore, drumming with her wings a sound like the surf, ruffling her feathers like foam.

Beating the air into an east wind, rolling the sun up over her back, blowing the full moon like a bubble out of her wet mouth, a cinder ring, a mirror. At the bottom of our steps, the gleam begins. I carry the fresh breeze to bed and wonder how to take the clay and make a sea angel with the moon on her tongue. How to take clay and make a path over the water.

Is it an angel, a bird, a holy gander, wild, who breaks the line of the shore? Is it death who breathes and sighs and surges there at the edge —death by drowning, drowning in the deep blue sea, the deep blue mother, the deep blue holy spirit realm, the unconscious consciousness? Through that barrier we pass like light, easy, and swim. What was that dream, and how do I make of clay a golden swimmer ... a school of fish ... schooling ourselves in the spirit waves, jumping the barrier?

How do we school ourselves in the real forms of what is true? The angel sips at our toes, drinks us in. Rolls us into the sun and we rise shining. How do we remember what it is to be human persons? Part of the sea, the sun, the moon. Human angels. How do we keep the faith with the clay and the fire, hearing the music, the ring and the roar? What it is to be clay and fire, we know that, in our bones and in our heart's desire. How do we keep the teaching straight: to enter into the consciousness of the clay, to unite with the fire? Governing with a wise hand, while the living form breeds in the molecules, while the life spirit readies its mineral garments, while spirit person prepares its new body in the heart of the vessel — the new body which quickens still as the pot breaks and falls away. Made of clay and fire, sea and salt, the vessel within the vessel — numinous origins of earthly elements. We are connected in our inwardness and tissue with the nature of things. We are not puppets and hirelings, nor circuitry nor systems. We are originators, warm with soul, in a gentle love-making with a double world: of sense and supersense. An ocean and an angel. A death and a life.

Words are spirits too, and the world is a temple, a temenos, a sacred precinct: invisible geometric forms, cathedral arches and porticoes, rose window mandalas, choral sounds and color tones. The poetry we human beings feel is written across the threshold. Ordinary consciousness, half awake, is only half the story. Remember the angel and the deep and the human vessel of clay that rides the waves.

2.

On Valentine's Day, I took a five-pound ball of clay out into the back garden protected from the wind, slapped it into a disk about seven inches across and two inches thick, shaped the disk into a heart, and began to pinch. First I marked out with my eye on the surface the figure I would pinch around, a heart-person, stretched in the four directions rising out of the opened clay, stretching out of it, into it, a continuum. A heart-clay-person rising out of the center and stretching to the periphery, rising out of the periphery and streaming into the center. I worked for an hour or so before I was to drive my friends to their houseboat. Millie came out of the studio. "What is that you're making there? Oh, your heart pot of course. It looked to me like a pelvis." A pelvis! How fabulous! More than I could have hoped for or claimed! In the evening, I worked more on the piece, smoothing, keeping the whole vessel heart-shaped, working the cruciform image free from the floor of the pot, arching across the space. At the lower point of the form, I opened it again to make a space below the skirt of the figure. Its attitude seemed oriental, leaning, swaying, a feminine aspect as well as big muscular arms and a chest all heart. A visitor came. "What's that?" "It's a wall piece," I said, "a heart figure — I like to work out of the festivals of the year." "Oh," she said, "I thought it was a fish." "It is," I said. A fish! How fabulous! More than I could have hoped for or claimed. I went to where she was sitting and looking at the form horizontally, right into the opening at the lower apex. "It is a fish's mouth," she said. "Or the whole thing looks like the skeleton of a fish head, with big eye holes. Upside down it looks like a crucifix." Wow. She was feeling it and touching it.

The next morning I went out to look at my piece, to work on it some more. I looked at the fish's mouth. I decided to close it and to extend the length of the figure to the point of the rim. But I'm glad to know it is there, agape. Agape, *agape*: change the accent and it is the Greek word for unpossessive love. The merciful fish.

3.

Clay, words, and creativity go together with a natural affinity. United at the root, they are born separately into consciousness, like the fingers of a hand. The mobility of clay, the meaning of language, the fruitfulness of creativity — these emerge from a common matrix, a deep sea mother — a spirit root —logos, a feeling for wordness, for form, for flowering. And so it must be, for an ancient syllable underlies them all, *bhel:* "To blow, swell; with derivatives referring to various round objects and to the notion of tumescent masculinity." Think of it: the gesture of swelling out, rounding out, being fruitful, blossoming, blooming, the form of a bowl, a bull's balls, a bellows, breath.

While I was living at Stony Point, New York, years ago, with Karen Karnes, David Weinrib, John Cage, David Tudor, I had an important dream. I was writing *Centering*. In my dream, I was talking with John and David, who are musicians. John was drinking a glass of water. I was telling him the "subject" of my work. He was saying, "There is no subject, everything is the subject." I became angry and replied that I had a particular subject that was not "everything is everything," and with that I knocked the glass out of his hand. Immediately, it sprang back, or another that looked the same with the same water in it, sloshing back and forth — the crystal, transparent, again in his hand, as if by magic. I started to walk away. David Tudor said, "I can help you with your work." I was very surprised. "Yes," he said, "I am clairvoyant about the future of society. It hangs upon linguistics."

Linguistics! I told the dream to my friend, the poet Charles Olson. "Take it as a directive," he said.

In the roots of words themselves are clues to the integrating sources of our humanity. To meaning. To connecting. To the word that underlies all vocabulary, which we experience when we experience the swelling out of the bowl, the ball, the bloom. We enter the realm of formative forces which create the physical forms, the language. We cannot see it with our eyes. Only the skin of clay that stretches it out, the petals it calls into being. But with the inner eye of intuition, of imagination, yes we know we are in that ongoing world of fruitful swelling in the continuum of seasons. The way our fingers belly out the bowl, as we pinch the pot or throw the clay on the wheel: this is archetypal, it is a primal gesture, it lives in our being, beyond this piece or that, this rose or that. As we live more consciously in the realm of these etheric gestures, we develop a clairvoyance for what is going on within, underneath, what is bringing something into being, what is coming into being, how it is in nature, in us. As we behave toward nature, we are behaving toward ourselves.

The more questions we ask about art, the more surely we transcend the canvas or the cup, the more surely we come to the spirit in activity, to inspiration, connection with living gestures and imaginations beyond pot-sherds and scaling paint. And the more questions we ask about spirit in activity, the more surely we walk right out the back door of birth and the front door of death and find that we sail through those gates like light.

The clay of ourselves changes as we grow and develop, become aware, undertake transformation, self-knowledge, ordeal by fire. Who is changing? Who is the changer? Who is dreaming my dreams? Starting with the syllable that underlies the bowl, the blossom, the testicle, we find our way to an identity that is not so simple as we thought: to an I and a me: to an individuality ongoing in the primal world of spirit substance and a personality hard

32

at labor in this passage of time and earth, refining its ores, modeling its form, filling its transparency with air, its silica sheath with all the colors of the rainbow. The glassblower's dance. The potter's eucharist. Transubstantiation. What else would it be?

4.

I sing the Barite rose from Oklahoma: a stone that grows in the shape of a rose. A stone grows. A rose forms. The myth speaks out, telling how the opposites marry. The stone and the rose, the shore and the sea. The mystical rose. The fire and the rose are one, as T.S. Eliot writes in his *Four Quartets*. Rose, lotus, chakra, spirit flower, the opening way, you bloom in the stone, the mineral body. A fruitful swelling. Stoneware. The stone and the bowl. The Holy Grail, thought to be a flat stone, receives the blood of the lamb, the living water. The philosopher's stone, agent of transformation sought by medieval alchemists, itself a fusion of the opposites: lead and gold, form and freedom, gravity and levity, dense root and light-filled calyx, matter and the tone that rings through it, per-sonnatus, "to be sounded through," person, stone rose.

Yes, this is firm ground here: inwardness extended throughout the body of earth and cosmos. Clay and consciousness.

5.

Sitting here on the steps of the studio, pinching a pot, experiencing a feeling that is full, but not emotional in any particular way. Some transformation has taken place. It is a sweet feeling, filling this bowl as it pinches itself into a curved plane. A fullness like the sun, the salt sea, warmth, empathy, to be offered. The emotional body transformed. Those old alchemists are our teachers. Clay and its transformations, if we experience them deeply, are mystical fact.

Oriental philosophy talks about the koan that asks us to hear the sound of one hand clapping, or nirvana that is empty of desire. Western meditation teaches us to experience the mind consciously and to focus; then to distance ourselves from the mind, to empty it. To empty the ear, so that we can hear. But first to experience the ear inwardly, in meditation, to develop a feel for what "hearing" and "listening" are — to get in touch with the spiritual sense organ, so to speak. The koan/nirvana/meditation practice is this bowl, brimming with emptiness: air, breath, light. With presence, with capacity. We experience inwardly the fullness of this light-filled emptiness. We practice centering the opposites, inside/outside, rose/stone, not leaving anything out, embracing, yielding. We practice our listening, our not-doing, wu wei, our receiving, our trust. Yes, this dark pot, this filament of clay, through which the quick of life makes its earthly run. A symbol, gathering place for the word that is no word. To feel the immensity of the small: the immensity of the experiences of pottery, what an integrating divinity it is: integrating, centering.

Personality is like the clay, given, but raw and unformed.

Form is an inner Being. It wrestles with thickness and weight —thins the walls, gives firmness and substance, lifts the rim, extends, shapes, in a generous curve. Like a pivot it corrects any one-sidedness. Less light, more weight. Less flow, more boundary. Less control, more source. Our two arms are stretched like wings from the pivot, centering all extremes, bringing in, integrating into the core, letting the new forms be born out of this wholeness now, the next wholeness to come. We are where we are, we clay angels, and our tone rings us round; farther we reach than we can see; we extend like the living vine, invisible before birth, carrying the lifelight like a miner's cap, through the crossing point. Our imagination already extends us into our next season of growth. Our intuition tells us to keep faith with the cracks, the droughts, the withering — to go the cosmic serpent's path — the coiling clay — never straight on. The next frustration may strike the brightest spark.

6.

... Make a heart vessel that contains the lies, the handicaps, the fears. Make them visible. Do not turn away. They are our companions, they are in us. Serve them. Include. Heal.

To make visible: epiphany! To cause to appear! To bring to light!

Isn't this what we try to do in our artistic work with the clay: to bring something to light, to manifest, to reveal? A form, an intention, a question, a relationship, a search, a hope, a defeat, a concealment ... ?

The sixth of January is the Christian festival of Epiphany: Three King's Day, when the holy child is made visible to the Magi. On this day I made a clay piece: a human figure reaching out from a center to the four directions, born out of the cup of the earth mother, born out of her fruitful swelling —and its limbs and head relink with the clay, stream back into the dust, filling it with human aspiration, with the possibility of human freedom.

The Epiphany of our clay is a paradox: so vulnerable, so breakable, such a perishable sheath. And having taken form, so form-transcending, so ensouling — both child of earth and its redeemer.

That inner spaciousness we feel is the form that we have created with our hands, and it spreads in waves through all the other things we touch.

Now it is Mardi Gras, Lent, and the preparation for Easter. Let the clay stir like sap, let it wait, and, in the emptiness of the stoneware tomb, a clay feather floats. Clay rags, clay dawn, clay voices — the new shape is forming — clay fired in the sun, nailed and torn, clay that doesn't quit —clay the anointed.

I made a sorrowing mother paten, her breasts like cut fruit, her child slack and sleeping. I made the font, "Forgive them father for they know not what they do" — and the last words, "It is finished," a clay cry.

These planetary festivals, winter solstice and spring equinox, festivals that grind our clay with the tides, are just the right size for potters.

To teach is to show. A showing is a revelation of more than we can see with our physical eyes; it shines into our understanding, *schön*. The beautiful is that which is revealed. And what is revealed?

> gold lustre swimmers and copper red fish
> angel nibbling at the shore
> and our clay feet walking on water

Wednesday of Easter Week

Sings the phoebe—
Draws the muskrat his paths
    through reeds in dark
    brush strokes—
Shakes the pussy willow its
    gold mane—

Weave these their net to catch
    the god falling into life.

Good Friday Athlete

How cunningly you, Christ,
    dodge the ultimate blow —
the knockout meant for you
on the cross nailed. But you knew
the secret way to your Father.
You played the game,
you yielded to the thorns, the spear,
the vinegar, the taunts and scorn —
they thought they had you caught and killed.

    So deftly you ran the field,
slipping just out of reach, into the tomb
and out again. You knew the earth
needed your blood and you gave it, a birthing pool:
the slow crawl onto the breast of time
and prophecy fulfilled.

    On this Good Friday the measureless leap
begins. A rainbow drained of color is the bridge,
an arching void, the landing still to shine
on Easter dawn.

How glorious is our vision of your body
hurtling through tides of time
and timelessness!

"I Thirst"

"I thirst":
          For what do you thirst, oh bird,
on your terrible tree? We feel your passion
spilling still. We too hunger, bird,
toward ecstasy. Oh to be known, received,
held as in a cup of arms,
a body cup waiting to be taken up.

I thirst.
This hungering for human love (I learn from you)
this hunger is divine, its terror sacred.
Oh dreaded touch!
Your flesh and blood
at our soul's mouth, Oh grail,
oh cup. We drink the earth,
we eat the sun.

How starved I am
and mad with drought; appalled
by passion's smouldering flame,
ashamed to feel how fire leaps in my womb
at the forbidden door.

Ah how I am then thunderstruck
to hear you cry your thirst:
behold you transformed thus
to bread and wine. "Come,
feed on me in your heart." Hunger
(you proclaim it) is divine, is
breast and hands, thighs,
and wilderness of appetite, is
godlust burning in us. We dare not
do without. Oh Christ
in your sunbright realms you
celebrate these shadows of desire,
they keep your passion true.
"I thirst," you cry, "come feed."

Hunger leads us to the feast:
life's awful beauty strangles in our throat,
tenderness empties us into pain.

Wait. Love's hunger is divine.
A god
        creates it.

Pelted by Beauty
(after an American Indian Flower Ritual)

The power of love received in the body: This was the Festival!
     how we stood and faced one another
       and we took hands
       and the love came.
     And all the flowers swarmed about our heads:
       deep deep the sting goes.
Let love be welcomed the moment it seeks us.

In my flesh I feel it still,
    the surprise and awe, the joy,
  warming and swelling in my limbs and belly,
    O miraculous conception O angels tumbling through the air!
How real it is, the Christscript branded across our lips:
    that we shall love one another — as if the world could ever be the same.
    Over the edge, into the well, the abyss,
        idiotically amorous,
    nibbling at the green fronds and flinging them!
Pelted by beauty and peace,
    a cellular reordering, each tiny vessel
    lovecrazed, opening.
The fountain erupts, cascades,
and we wish to die in it, be other,
be one in an alchemy of eros,
that lad with the arrows who shoots blind.

The power of love is received in the body,
    our first and primal home.
Not enough is made of incarnation, the mysteries of birth,
    of embodiments here like this *in* one another:
      your eyes and my arched back,
        our fingers softening.

Of course now we dance differently,
    bowing and dipping and turning to the delicate drum.
Of course we live now in the dread of our disguises.
    We know our body and offer it,
  We know our need and carry our begging bowl.

Now hear with courage our own love cries,

the tender shout of readiness, yes,
I will, I do, yes, let us receive into our bodies
    the divine pulse, anointed with petals,
awaken and go forth changed.
                          Now truly are we god's fools,
lilies of the field, no thought for the morrow,
feeding strangers and comforting the fearful,
doing good to those who hurt us,
carrying blossoms to beat beauty and peace into our bones.

This poem was written October 13, 1989 after a ceremony in which this ritual was performed. At its climax, a huge basket of flowers was poured over the poet's head, engulfing her in their multifloriate rapture. It was she who was being celebrated in this ritual, and it was she therefore who had to be most deeply pelted, nay, pulverized by beauty! It was a magical ecstasy, moving, as the poem sings, through the body into a new behavior.

Love Poems

"I believe the appropriate symbol of the cosmic Christ who became incarnate in Jesus is that of Jesus as Mother Earth crucified yet rising daily."
—*Matthew Fox*

"Jesus is our true Mother in whom we are endlessly carried and out of whom we will never come."
—*Julian of Norwich*

Deep Ecology

Christ's blood is green
    in the branches,
blue in the violet.
    Her bright voice
laughs in the night wind.
    The big nova swells
in her breast.
    Christ suckles us
with spring sap and
    spreads earth under our feet.

O she loves us,
feeds us, tricks us with
her triple ways:
calls us soul,
calls us body, and spirit.
Calls us to her bed.

Liturgy

O I touch and am touched
by the smouldering core of you.
The colors that surface in your flesh
carry my sight into the temple beyond seeing.
My heart is pounding, impatient for the sacrament
that changes our bodies into communion.
You are my door. Through you
               I am entered.

A Westerner Visits Australia

Aphrodite lifts her foaming mouth to the beach
and steps from her shell. We fly
in a microscopic plane
through plankton and salt
to the mother-lode-Uluru:
red rock, old rock, deep rooted,
honey combed patterns
in the caves of our birthing.
Ochre overlays, spirals, and effigies,
O ancestor, blow on my hot feet your talisman waters —
O goddess of love refashioned!

Aphrodite, you live still in the blister of water
on the aboriginal frog, to be opened
when our thirst mounts. You live
in the wild fig, the grub, the honey ant.
    Bloodwood, bright sap, red mother rock,
running colors in the wandering seas of the sun.

We come with our stories of love
to this rock of abandonment:
the alchemists' rock, womb
of renewal — the old goddess watches us
peel away our bark, our covering, our protection.
    How shall we love
before we have lost everything?
Then the green shoot in the wasteland,
the footprint in the mud of the bushwalk —
gratuitous, for even our hunger is gone,
razed by the fire at the center.
    Only the veiled eye of the frog,
    the eroded escarpment.

The walkabout consecrates our nakedness to her kiss.
Yes, Aphrodite of the walkabout,
blackened and lustrous,
sing your song lines, your dreaming:
the latticework beneath the surface,
network of dancing, holding, and letting go.

Captain Bligh and Captain Cook
searched these waters
and found their treacherous channels.
We walk through their shadows into the rainforest of Bruny
and fall down at her feet
who blesses the journey in our tiny craft
sailing her waters.
          There is a camp here in the maelstrom,
and tomorrow landfall,
and the next day EASTER,
when we-Aphrodite, a radiant vortex,
wet with our tears the feet of love
and dry them with our hair.

The Shaman Comes Home

for Joan Halifax

Comes home, she comes . . .
following a maze of bone seeds crystalline,
spelling her new becoming.

Dismemberment, and all her parts
boiled and eaten — scoured and stripped,
beside herself (ecstatic!) with singing —
singing the wild lullabyes of the entrails
in the smiling blue serene.

Her moon nature is sunlit — the phallus
rises in her womb — O androgyne,
an intimacy beyond gender! O terror of transformation!

Whatever beast or bird has carried her,
whatever raging snake has spat its hate,
through her crazed essence play
the sacred drum, the raven's whistle,
the twitter of dancing beads.

Sunk in filth, in visions entranced,
her skeleton dresses again its flesh
for the brisk waking.

—comes home, she comes
    to the trees and mice
    the streets and houses.
Now forever sick and wounded she is,
forever broken and whole —
dead and alive, readied
for the rituals of love:
sucking the sick breath, kissing the awful sores,
dancing the illness and its mystical core.

Comes home, she comes:
to answer the mail
do the laundry
bury the garbage
dust the books

lay the fire
cook the rice
climb the mountain
plant and gather
sleep and wake
quake and weep
— to live the world
    she has become.

Early Poems

1945 - 1960

Elegy for My Father

Do not tremble, the leaves will set
will set;
gone black, gone blind,
gone dead—gay dog—will drop.

There, do not tremble, heart's heart,
    unhearty undoughty heart, sound
        as a celery root:
the leaves, on the trees, will burn, up,
the dead ash will last, to spring, up,
and all's a bright dying.

One two three four   death's a march.
Repeat, rags for flags,
Toss, in the fall of fire, toss
and fling up
your dying — break, from the branch,
break out. Dry, all over the wise old ground.

Death's a march.   Hup!
Round and down our roads and hills
Formations drill. Splendid!
It's there for you to finger, to frame,
It's everywhere to name: Sir,
        silly sweet babe
        silly sweet babe.

Lie quiet, stir, drop, gold leaf
by leaf our childish store
and spend time
— o do not reel so, heart — adore
the unicorn's thin templet
make much
        of spying

Ars Poetica

That particular what. That.
The particular roots in a round land,
a lordly gardening plot, room to the all of us.
Where it goes, grows under all of us.
So with any one and wonderful thing. It's all's in its somehow.

But, to be born is particular.
The navel is a thing, I think. Linkentwining
    cable of allflesh. But a; I think of it as,
All's sign. Ours.
So why's what I without thinking about it shout about it, this,
    that, your particular radiance? Man's, that's found.

Then: and the sight of one, hand to a trowel,
    making spring do right by turnip greens
and my wren's throat a-shake with its outcry:
                :luv o my luv my lord and luv
                take o take me to you, resting hand,
                stark and naked on my soul, blue bole and bellyfull
I am witless with my singing as birds are
for mate and mist for all the salty springtime
and that particular flickering high flight;
as they are, for the rite.

Oh satisfy yourselves that this particular way of mine
is sign is signal single
whole,
That this any psalm, or canticle, for any this man
Happens,
And all's its double trust.

Place Is the Soul's Planting

Blue strikes like the head of a match,
the blue line spins from post to pile
while the blue bird flies. No wake.
Plunderer of the deep well, I tell you, bird,
your color skyed my earliest fountain,
your thin blue spell opens the eyes I dream of.
Run away run away to Charleston, play with no more birds, and
wisely:
I tell you we are hell bent.

And why is room the same in Charleston: moon
sea struck together in the same deep well
that home forever knows: my lake at home takes
its moon nightly. The sweeter southern air bares me.
O how is it my lady moon that you lie with the sea?
Run farther still

into southern spring. Forget all myths of fate fled
to be met elsewhere, forget deceit
plunging elsewhere. I tell you we must guard
though the garden has its gate. I think I have passed for a stranger
when the thundering thicket of passion
blasted in bloom bends to me. Your nails have a long bite.
I handle the terrible trees, move in the flowers' throats
nose and mouth, bunch and break the piling purpling fruit,
dirty myself with pollen, and say nothing: dared,
destiny deals in metaphor;
assaulted I suck the stem and wish its honey bitter.
O unrelenting why to woo the fate we fall to.

Now symbols tell the tale:
bird sea moon and nerveless bloom make irony.
Crater it where the deep well gains
and love you the legend : place is the soul's planting,
carry it we will carry it and dwell there.
Destiny who keeps the lodging names us,
the myth is true.

November

The sun is melting in the sky
and the black branch mints few gold leaves now.

Two Portraits

Charles Olson

specifically talking, I
mean the words he uses or
rather utters — salivates, for
instance, is what he does with the
image to home it, what is it, it's
homing, it's a homer. Big to the eyes,
of all,
higher than the eyes and wider
than / spaced: specks, 'stache, bobs
off his words with his incisors / breathes. In.
Huff, and pow-nd, puh-ress, plunks out
bass. Gnash, or bucket up
the swim. Goh on, you're, are you, abs-
olutely right I'll buy that. Stems up!
Eyes
oh-pen!

After Seeing Sybil Shearer Dance ...

Did the dancer flit?
She flat.
And I bravoed the where
she hath not sat.
6 yards of tulle, a peck
of plush, and 3
bare feet, rubberized.
Soul full, she pricketh the air
with her toe, and
noddeth to God.

Winter Poems

the snow is white and pink
                    and   i think
                of your   dink-
        y ears

the snow is white and pink and green
                        like ice cream
and blue too, except blue is hardly ever in ice cream
except around the edges of black-raspberry

and the stream is brownish and greenish
like a toad or a frog, that color like a tree
which you don't know what color it really is
but it looks like wood, only the stream is
moving and gliding and running and making big bodies
brownish and greenish and yellowish in the snow and ice.

Seasons seem not in sequence but in layers,
or something like that: this morning I went out to my automobile
in the early light of day, lots of ice and snow,
and although it was dawn it was silent and still
and yet in that stillness I thought of the birds I would hear
when spring comes. I didn't think about them wishing I could hear them now
but rather really hearing them in the depths, at the center,
of that dawn sound, which to the outer ear seemed soundless
but to the inner was full of birds as well. Like a transparency
of spring over the hoosh of winter.
I have this feeling with people when I look at them,
seeing in the child her summer and autumn,
in the summer man his spring and winter; in
the gasping day the crack of dawn.

Winter.
All the twigs in the world are
in my eyes.
Through this forest of twigs I see
an ice heart damaged
in the alive onrushing brook;
gold and ice, a heart descended. I lie
to the touch of the ice heart descended

and gouge the formful skin of winter.
I adore, and gouge it rough shod through the winter.
The heart turns transparent where it touches.
My cat melts beside me
to whiskers and eyelashes, pounces
unshod on phantoms, . . . winter
falling . . . and . . . splashing.

March

the blood is climbing up the tree

        it sings to me
        it sings to me

the drop has flown

        what can I see
        what can I see

a web
a fist
a spectral hand

        brimming to life
        invisibly

April

I

piping peepers
poke a hole in silence,
tweet, shooing spring with whistles

II

wake robin, rue,
fiddlehead, curly dock.
what luck! spring's.

III

Suddenly the moon
buttons fast our hill
to the the night.

IV

Moonshine
hangs night on a twig.
Its green shadows make leaves
everywhere.

V

A dogtooth violet
has a throat big as a canary's
5 fangs, 2 shoulder blades,
reversible hood —
catches my eye, eats my heart.

Three Songs

Aria

I love your rose hips and your vines.

●

Song

Sage,
myrtle and liver wort,
my love lives by green leaves, and roots and, seeds.

●

Song

Though separated, we see the sun set and the moon rise
as if by arrangement.

A Black Swan

A black swan has a red mouth.

Poems from Poems

1947

Imagine Inventing Yellow

Imagine inventing yellow or moving
For the first time in a cherry curve.

What Imagination Means

Across the Golden Gate from San Francisco
Between the bay and the Pacific
Lies Marin County.
                    When I was living
In Berkeley I would sometimes spend Sunday
Walking across the ridge above Muir Woods
Between Mill Valley and Stinson Beach.
                                 Once
I walked washed there in empty air and heard
Between the ocean's grand oblivion and
The white stair of the city one small bird
Sing, all prodigal, to his bare theatre.
                               Since
He inhabits my mind high on a wire and
Wonders me what imagination means.

Words like Windows Mirror You in Distances

Words like windows mirror you
like windows dimly mirror you
in distances
like distances you view

Look through.

Surfaces hang everywhere like picture planes:
pane of water, skin of leaves,
time on chromium and stone,
space felt against mountains and the roaming armor of seas;
    surfaces, we love each other.

Words can be voyage through.

I like to think of poetry as window
I like to say:
this way like magic steps you through
your own dim image into life.

O bright self you did not know you wear the sun so well.
O roads of destiny you run through me.
Wilderness my world, roses and fire my vision too,
dimensions of words you outdistance me.

By sculpture clumsy tools mark through to wonder.

Words like windows mirror you
like windows dimly mirror you
in distances.
Words carry distances to you.

Alchemy

Facts drop down
Like lead through our nerves' funnel. One
Who wonders runs her feeling
Round their edge:

> When my mother died,
> her mouth fell open.

> Five years later my father
> dropped ashes in the Columbia River
> from a bridge
> called The Bridge of the Gods.

Now I in alchemy
Here feel her shock,
His turning wrist intolerably,
Their letting go.

Now I may claim the gold from clay:
Years ago today I looked
And limped away; in my breast's alembic
Cupped the foolish face.

There cinders swung
Hot in the current of my grief,
Mixed with his fingers' slow relief.
Agitation rocked its vessel, clung.

Say imagination is my crucible:
Say in this tender, deeply torn,
The elements exchange occasion
For a sense; their last expenditure.

This miracle of change we seek,
The chemistry of meaning we employ;
We reach for mystery and touch the heart,
Converted with the pain, our joy.

Lover's Fate

My bird, my pet
My tenderer yet
Than shoot, than leaf
My heart, my love
My thickly stirring light above
The joy, among the grief

Sing here, curl here
Stir smoothly near
This mouth, these hands.
Bring blood, bring hate
For lovers' fate
Of vapor and of sands.

Late Augury

Late augury,
how do the portions lie?
Will the wind change, will it blow rain
and my love green again?

I'll dance for drops,
bright augurer, I'll spring
when the green grows, and the grain
of my love is full again.

In New Orleans

In New Orleans there is a great deal of iron work,
iron at balcony edges, iron work latticing in.
In my heart in New Orleans there is no balcony
and hardly any iron work.
There is one large high-ceilinged room,
no furniture to speak of. There are a bed and a mirror.
In the old quarter of New Orleans everything
is pretty well run down, over with, antique.
My heart was such a graveyard once
and you caretaking carried it high-stepping over history.
New April in New Orleans is very ceremonial,
gentiles and jews doing the rites of ambivalence.
I listen to the bells of Holy Thursday and
I see us in our heart-shaped room create the Easter myth.
Eastertime in the French quarter in New Orleans. The heart is loam
and I move between death and spring because it is natural.

To Hate the Sun

When the sun comes down to earth, so to speak,
we get into it.

When the sun lies long against the ground and gets warm into it
then we come out of the rooms and lie down,
bandaged here and there like warriors.
When the sun comes warm clear down to the ground
then we crawl on our bellies or backs or otherwise into it.
When it comes down hard
touching beyond equivocation
when it is not lost head-high in air
when the sun comes down hard enough to mean spring
then it invites us into it as it invites the leaf out of its dark twig
and pigment pleads its passion in the sun.

I know and reknow this every year.
But now I sing a different song of O for the summer color, for
seated against some sandy wall
fitting through rays, spitted in flame
captured by warm insistence and the
pleasure
of an even burning turning
darker
launched in light I looked, and found (struck sight) a black girl;
she swung her shining eyes
and irony spread in me like a natural blight.

Is it a standing joke for Negroes I have never heard,
what did Narcissa think when she passed by
and what am I to think when I
lie thoughtlessly turning black
in the summering sun.

You cannot catch the beetle bitter smack in the eyes
of Negroes, I know,
you cannot dare the diffidence and their fear
nor fret to fracture the genteel plane they offer you
to chink their light and darkness through,
you won't live by this and like as well the good weather and the leaves.

And so we lose what I have always wanted
and felt close to in the spring. Don't talk to me about
the race problem:

To hate the sun

Organization

Organization is not interesting, why.

If I am the chairman and you are on my committee it is not very interesting.

Or if you are the leader and we are your group and stay so who isn't bored.

Organization is all right while it is new until you thoroughly understand
what is expected of you and then what is expected of you
is soon no longer interesting.
It gets to be like a minuet or a masque that isn't play any longer but
the whole show.

Some people like to know what is expected of them and what
the consequences will be but not me.

Some like to set themselves goals and be clear about aims so that they can
formulate standards and have an institution to which they can feel they
belong

But I don't want to belong to an institution.

Organization is not interesting but sometimes necessary to get things done
if there is something that simply must get done and better done wrong
than not done at all, are there such things maybe.

Governments are well organized but the people in the governments
do they see it all so clearly, who makes the policy and is he well organized
with the right leadership and support or is he a house divided.

Organizations and institutions and government are not interesting to me
and perhaps that's not important

But I see more and more people expecting from them whatever they are
benefits they would not expect from any of the men composing them,
I mean what rare bliss will organized humanity bestow that a man will
not give his brother.

When I was a child I liked to be a member of a gang and have a leader
and a code and meetings and by-laws and a constitution and a declared
purpose and a stern loyalty to our side. What was good was that this

public life instructed me privately in the possibilities of attitudes.
But as I grew and filled the rooms inside me I found the converse true:
public life became a mirror. And so to play with governments
is to toy with mirrors rather than with men.

Will my bold anarchic dream come true and we will govern ourselves
unprofessionally, mirroring as universe our heart's terrain.
The private world is where men meet. It is much more interesting to look
than to see what is not there.

For Political Reasons

The way a man eats is political.
For political reasons is for human reasons, confidence vote is
        not entirely politic.
We fired a man from our faculty one year
and students of course asked why. For political reasons?
If for political reasons unfair.
If for political reasons, then unjust, was it for political reasons.
Yes if politics are in the house, if they live across the cove then
        no.
No if politics is party, if the way a man governs himself
        yes only then.
I find it hard to answer honestly with care those who ask
is it for political reasons because I think about it differently:
I don't think politics when a man intimidates, I think human;
what he conceives politically grows face and hands,
image of government is self-portraiture.
I don't see departments, I see whole and I see features
some of them maybe political, pressing it outward.
Fruit grows on a tree, unless my eyes deceive me.
If I don't trust a man, his politics are not the cause,
though they too stem from roots. So all I finally say is
yes and no. And I find more and more that I say more and more
        yes and no
when I am asked if I think something is true, because
I don't think of what is true as any phrase one safely keeps.
I don't think ever so well-chosen words are likely to do the trick
or knowledge is now our homing-pigeon home.
I think of continually circling about and edging in,
but I wouldn't care much for a truth that was
"for political reasons." It would be smaller than a man.

Poems from Centering

1964, 1989

Snow

White moths in crazy mobs
hunt everywhere
the flame of the winter sun.

That Supreme Point

Why is everything called
by another name:
water is smoky pearl this first bright morning of spring in the Mine-
       sceonga at a depth of 14 inches over granite
birds are flutes
grass is having its hair streaked
last week's sleds are beached in the field
it's all a big double-take, a dedoublement as the French say, a
       haunting:
the world is full of phantoms walking around in bodies.
The primal stuffing is leaking out all over the place,
it's bound to get mixed up either outside or inside human speech.
What's the difference, the sages spend a lifetime trying to get to
       that supreme point where
everything is everything else, and here it is happening down here
       on my level.

Touch-taught

Picks it up, the earth, and gives it to me.
He somewhere walking
and the feel of it: like tides
fingering up, the feel
feeds up me, me a shore, a rising ground.

The earth runs round,
is endless.
Even oceans hold in its folding plan
and acres that sink
climb dry again.

(There's philosophy in it.)

No brinks. No
far forever lost and fallen away with you.
Bear up, I. Retaliate with love.
The earth's turned round like a mill,
and slaves. Observe:

We blind and touch-taught. I catch,
I catch your print, imprint, your pressing,
here. Up my trunk like sap — wells brilliantly —
my coils, current; nerve it is.
Quicker at least I am.

O it's he somewhere a-walking, dear.
You man and we can be.
It's the clay claims us and the
        day that says stir and step out
He'll hear

Giant

A giant lives in a house of stone
and fishes all day in the pool off his porch
for gimcracks.

He keeps a wife
who grows cabbages for his
springtime meal.

I found him out by swimming
up the creek
and hanging on his pole
in the shape of a toy balloon.

Granted.

He took me up and laughed
and blew me into shape,
face and figure female.

All right. It was all right.

When we walk over the hills
I swing on his hip
like a saber swings,

and when we lie drinking
under the waterfall
he ties flies around me.

I tell you this giant
and I
make castles when we want to
of jasper and pearl.
And we fill them with sights
anyone would want to see.

We stir the stars about at night
to soften our bed

and he can clear the whole husky universe
with the light he carries.

The First Morning

The sun at the top of the hill
Fits its arm down my sleeve
And I run to you.

You pet me with your long light
And your white eyes dissolve into
Day.

Brightness falls through the air.
Where you are, dunes of gold
Tell the way.

Now sweeter than milk
On your breast I lie down,
A flower in your throat
My face to the sun.

To My Class at City College, New York

I am 65 years old and have no wisdom.
I LOVE YOU ALL, EACH ONE OF YOU.

Crushed
in a shining room your sweet sap
runs
berries goldenrod flesh and the flowing eyes
flush my face with their radiant spray

DRINK is the course it takes.

(I reel in the brimful sepulchre.
To be so devastated at your taste,
the single joy each one of you de-
clares in me. Thou,

my self, come to sense and soul
a tidal cup. I dash you to the wall
of the world, spill you green to
its halls.

Every other one I know

shines with your wetness like pebbles more themselves

in the sea, spirits drunk.

I owe you life.

Levity

Twelve sunflowers were in bloom this morning in my garden, eastbound

      brightly the animate disk lifts
    —the missionary tangle winds good up—
    in the soil, in the soul

    O
    this is
              the finest
w e a t h e r   w h e n
    gold dies, a finer alchemy,
    when gold's exchanged
                for the dingy
    seeds (bed down, life is with us),
    when the sun grows old, the glitter congeals,
    the damp warm bright pulp into bits and tatters,
    paper and splinters and rayless wheels.

    this is the finest weather ...
        glass eye scantily opens a cold mirror,
        shore winds, high tides of
falling color, troughs and palisades,
the gala inebriate storm ...

       (DECREASE and DELIVERANCE, how the oracle
       speaks:
       How days wane, the hallooing winter-ed solstice, the
       hanging bough fallow, unflowering, less.
       The increase of energy, the simple life, the
            spending out
                    of spirit.
                       DELIVERANCE
       DELIVERANCE
    o my soul
    o levity)

... ... the tide slipping,
        arms full still of summer and

the wine turns in your blood of dazzling daring dauntless dear
                    dear autumn.

        when gold prepares for death,
        perfects its seed, readies its force
                    for
                                the plunge
        airborne, earthborn, readies the nut
                    for
                                the next cycle.

Sun lustre flower, bright animate disk,
            most radiant in power
to perfect its grain,
            how beautiful we are!
preparing for death
                    the living seed!

Infancy limbwise and full of will
            pulls us against gravity erect
    tall grown in thought, in feeling bushed out,
    the splendid bright face blooms ...
                    darkens, shrinks
and life in us toils
                    to die pregnant
(we cannot kill ourselves, we can only sleep)
            and
by levity,
        rise starward, planetary, off earth.

Look at this garden: what an august fire
                            circulates
                            to be thus

                            entrusted (thank you sun wheel
                                    thank you seed flower
                                        seminal geometry
                                            fiscal rose)

            and this man:
Look how gloriously we bloom
        en route: the ovum charges, divides, extrudes, declares function,
                    declares heredity, hones its heavenly Excalibur on
                    the sands of time, in this house; brings

soul into being as sun is sucked out the green stalk
as the flower brings itself into being through the death of the
seed; we have no fathers and no mothers, are
not seedlings,
when, out of our brittle case we cast ourselves.

Look: light: ⎧ the air
                 ⎨ the harvest
                 ⎩ the spasm

Do You Realize Who We Are

Radio tubes are ringing it all in my ears.

Tune in on
NOTHING
astir with sound ...
magnetizing particles ...

FORM:

in a branch of electricity.

Contact with the sun
is about to be made.

If my ears can hear
the sound of the sun
I'll dress them
by god
and put them on the mantelpiece.

Ecoute — mes oreilles se dressent:
l'univers parle:
de l'amour?
de l'haine?

Don't be idiotic — the universe speaks of itself.
We find we are its vocal chords
brushed by breath
speaking our own name.

LISTEN! DO YOU REALIZE WHO WE ARE?

Hands

birds.

At Ground Level

Pots are for shards,
                        and
shards are
               for shepherds, to cry with.
SHAPES. taken, and taking
shape:
           avoid it if you can, you can't,
           shape's the void
           we're in; order is
           the chaos we befriend.
                            SAMSARA: one
thing and not another, one thing
and then another; samsara, is what
it's called, what we're at and what we're
in: forms, and naming. Names we bandy and
are scouted by, th'outs and innings, everyday a
requiem-birthday,
                    spilling the shepherd's tears,
                    spoiling the shepherd's fears —
                                   JOB,

the job's
           permanent
at ground level.

Sea Speech ... the Gulf Stream

for Owen Barfield

nature and spirit
the word incarnate

AI YA   AI YA   the green rigmarole, señor!
sea; wind; semaphore, of gulls. The
green
rag rustles, and abides. The
lime-lit decimal multiplies. REAP
the blue grain, DECANT:
decant th'Imperial flame.

I see that the sun is a red berry.

Oceans, of oceans, I
        cannot enumerate, nor re-
peat, measure nor cast, to count. Even
in this Caribbean crib, Nature you
are so busy. Changing everything.
Even here where it is still.

NATURE! her spittle, on the beach, her
salty tongue
                roping out rocks,
her edge —
            lessness, her
                    logos —

fleshed out: in, stands of sponges;
honeycombs for coral bees; gagging cranes;
whey at shallows; pelicans asprawl; ...
her logos,
        is it meant to
                    silence, us?

(white wands and streaming willows, catch syll-
ables; stone fret, hard and hollow towns
and towers — exultancy snaps
my bill! I fish, for words: still

89

screaming, die
                in praise — "you
can't do better than that, amigo"
                                [but
who's doing it — wait
!I've something to tell you ...])   :

    the ocean's belly dance, its lover hovering horizonwide
    hangingfire shippingwater against her
    till flush he falls, and the dark, to lock
    in love, with light
    indistinguishable, the full dish of earth,
    the dawn of
                a NEW
    day:
                I give you the new born, the never yet, lived, the
                not yet, dead, the
                vocative 'declare yourself' DAY:
                                            NATURE, dearest,
    collaborator, the picture we make!: our
    child, shining, spills; creates space; spurts, red;
    drills; and by our dance, keeps time
    ticking — hear the starboard swell click on th'hour,
    hear me trip, and reel, swinging my lariat:

    Light makes Us one, oh MOTHER, SISTER, HUSBAND, VOID!
Voices, we marry, and unite.
                        Our light originates
in us.   See how we wave.
        See how
    I am
        the thickening of light, its
    trajectory ...
            (how it escapes, like steam
        See how you, Mother, nurse at my breast
        See
            OUR seed shapes
)
(ah
 antiphony, my voice
without, your note's
                inaudible)

Envisioning

. . . . the Christ Within: what a beautiful thought!
The warmth and light and love radiating from within,
the fountain, the freshets of spirit-person,
my limbs of the tree of life, my muzzle in the waters of life,
my udder swinging and banging with milk and honey,
and Krishna riding herd on me as I find the holy river of mother earth
and Shiva opens his third eye and Cyclops loses his one,
and one from three leaves two, created by the light of the world
in order that they might see where they was at.

And I John saw the holy city, new Jerusalem, coming
down from God out of heaven, prepared as a bride adorned for
her husband.

The precious stones of her housing.
The mercurial lapis in which gold hangs.

The hermaphrodite, the rebis, artifex and soror, uroboros, the
self-generating impulse
        of which two sexes are our mutation,
and sacrament of marriage,
        the living seed in the magic vessel —
fire in the stone.

Recovery of the Child in Adulthood

... pick up the cord
out of the invisible, the visible
out of the dark, the light
out of the heavy, the light: the seed, the grape
                            the sand, the vine ...

In the heavy, hovers the youth's face,
hovering in this face, the child.
Out of the deep sea, the dark horizon, the sun
                                  dahlia
                                  sun-face, a
falling ball, in time, recovers its fire
to us; the falling hand, through time, and loss,
regains;
through all her dying seasons, nature
contracts, by law,
to bear
        seed/
                 as out of absence, the present;

plow/does not make life, only living/
                            brings to fruit
what ether bore.

As out of the sea, the thing that has been swimming,
as up the dark, the day: the thing
that has been swimming self-propelled
surfaces THERE:
                    prophetic infancy
we may recover

in this aging face, the child visible: here, just now,
as we raise our muzzle in the wind to
sniff
        (and the wind catches a side of your mouth
            and widens your throat and your eyes with breath
                and you cannot keep your laughter down for bodies don't lie
                    and the solar plexus expanding like the universe and
                        the child riding high, gleeful, until, shuddering with

fear and shame, we fall over the brink and darkness
films our eyes and our bones shrink back into place),
as we address ourselves, as
we point out. As in anxiety,
our prayer.
(With our first cry, the doom is set. Doleful,
we hang back. Aware, grin and gleam, picketing
our masters; guffaw and titter, tease the shadows to,
come to, and the night will fall as I must fall, and up the night
the strong muscle of sleep reaches to starry spheres. There is that
hope at least, that nature is stronger than our vanity, pull down
thy vanity, pull down
the set expression, the mineral glint.)

By the pall-bearers of our eyes, death
is carried out. Disciples in our eyes unmask. The
agile tongue,
                    O babyhood!   Flames
in our blood, the shrouding clouds invade, let
the bright spray play, the light strike, the
thunder clap, the weapons of speech sound arms for life un-
drowned, let the bright head move up and the stalk make way,
the mobile bloom climbs all the way,

          your face, grown friend, is beautiful
          I can see the child in it
          who is beautiful, who is being born, reborn,
          your face is buoyant with the soul in it who lives in it
          this soul leads the way

the aging heart recovers
                    flames
              in our veins, run
              their hot red track
EARTH   AIR   WATER   FIRE
          o alchemy, tricks
                    out a human of such sublime
              ingredients,
                        fierce
                                  industry, to whet
                                                  our
          bursting souls against the bark

93

               of time,
                      bring
             in our mortar
                         transformation.
      It is not then, it is not ever,
      it is just now, this moment, when
                       the priceless
     pearl
        is given.
                Look in the nacre and behold
the airy figures of what you have been and are yet to be.
Between dark and light the colors come.
Meta-
    morpho-
sis, thin and tensile stuff of worms and
butterflies, plays
        out perpetually
spun out, pick up the
           spectrum, see the
karma out, I see myself coming to meet me,
hail the phantom with an old hello, it is
my resprouting nature I resow
and harvest and resow,
          my seed I
             bless, pick up
the child
    who wept and leapt and dreamed of levitating worlds, wild
lilies of the field as prime, and elegant, alien and beloved,
exacting prototypes and images of what we are and are yet to be.
O fair fair, the splendor of it, in my mind's eye Horatio,
cruel and rigorous, lit with phosphorescence, an aura of supernatural
release, of all the sensual pleasures and all truths.
O happy fate, I cried, to be born in such a world.
At sunset, I can see it now, an attic window in an American suburb,
yellow frame, over the shingled roof, the opalescent run-off, the
gold and black colossal orbs, day and night, substantial; dreamed then
    grand savages, bare and always full of color,
sinuous, various, single total organism in motion and ensouled,
brought to salvation, saving their
gleaming skins, their enchanted bodies of light,
in light.
      How necessary it was in these worlds always to be at one's best:
one's warmest, noblest, most understanding, quietly persevering, healing,

how gracious it was, and perfectly aware of the difficulties and
the earnestness and the perils everywhere, perfectly
aware of how there are no alternatives to love and to danger, they are the
law.
        When one grew up, a poet and a missionary, one
would pack the pretty padded box the dress-up clothes were in
with food and gifts and go off to the east, whence
comforts do increase, as the bard says,
(and light does seize my brain with frantic pain, he continues,
when one is a little older). One would go among the heathen,
and have one's energies restored, one's clairvoyance reinstalled,
one's racial childhood reborn — and as new impulses stirred
up one's trunk, in turn one would lay one's hands on those beautiful
strangers and they would be healed by the human touch of personal love
and they would not be afraid to awaken into knowledge as it
unfolds from within, nor to enter into themselves. One would
bring the earth's being alive into their unearthly elements.
One would hazard all one's love in a single throw. Perpetually
hazarded, perpetually replenished. One would be freed by yielding.
One's better self would quest like The Pure Knight for Corbenic,
for talisman, leaving love a foaming wake of
questing. Ha, the myths and fairy tales, how they come alive,
out of childhood, how they come alive now in the adult, the
cinders and the peas, the sleeping beauty and the kiss that wakes,
the brutal slaying and the resurrected incandescent prince.
        The child saw the burnished columns ablaze,
felt the heat. Stand back! Stand aside!
Let truth be revealed! ... knew
all the world were members of the flames, signaling, signaling.
What a beautiful perilous physiognomy life has always had, no wonder one
falls in love at first sight.
                    Reached in her hood of fire,
reached in her nervous system and her bile,
found sound in the lyre her motions made,
felt the language organ grow and jut
between the vision and the ear, a golden walking cane,
a splendid fertile phallus, straightening, straightening.
    Knew as the splendid channel fed,
she was already dying; knew the kingdoms of this world
perpetually expire.
                    The scene unseen: trace
the vine, pick up
            the thread,

the magic is not in the mirror. Turn.

Ask the question. There is only one.
The king is maimed, and the land lies waste,
in a despairing emaciation of sap, the
vine! the vine!, the spellbound mind
is enslaved by its wounds, the
Pure Knight quests for his king, and he fails,
quest on, quest on,
the perilous rites must be performed.

    Entombed in the shadows, alone
with oneself, convulsed
in ordeals of terror and shame, grief-
scourged, aghast, one persists,
battles perdurable foes:

                Penetrates, penetrates
       to the invisible sheath of the source of the life of the light
         of the darkness of the self in the transparent body
            of warmth and of motion
               and inner equilibrium self-indwelling, one's matter
                  is one's home, one's heart is one's dove, one's love
                 is one's companion,
one's odyssey in time
            returns. Telemachus my son,
            my old nurse knows me by my stains,
            my flaws connect me everywhere,
            I still the wonder on her lips.
            My wife, my son, my dog, all imperilled
in my absence, I reclaim
            against perdurable adversaries!

Earth's fallen kingdom contains its original face.
Genesis peeps
through the orbiting scrawl of nuclear worlds,
seedbeds in their splintering rays,
dazzling playgrounds at the centers of darkness:
the carousel twirls, the calliope twangs,
angelic demons sparkle and brood in spasms of will.
Celestial glimpses
    in the
            infernal force.

The figure persists.

It reclaims, at the source, the flow.

In the darkness a second birth wakes,
the question rises with mounting energy
out of absence
    speaks the knight, the voyager,
    the wasted realm:
        "KING,
            YOU
            ARE MY BURNING QUESTION.
            YOU
            ARE THE FLAME, YOUR
            SUFFERING
                    ENGULFS ME, OUR
            FIRES
                    TAKE FIRE."
        And the king says, "I am healed."

        "King,
            whatever I behold
            is the flame, it
            is the burning question of life and death.
            I enter it, I ask
                    the question, I am
            consumed."

        And the king says, "You have overcome death."

The metabolism of daily fare turns
    water into blood, bread into body, we
        celebrate communion with
the dead; who are the dead? what is your death? what death lives in you alive
and waits to dwell outstandingly?
                    Initiation is death.
                    Acts decay. Death prospers,
                    nature asks: across the threshold
                    carry the thread.

Carry the throes, sweetest rapture of dearest love
    the blissful pulse of life given to, lover I come and I spend
my passion and my grace in you, life lover no end of spouse

97

in the fragile merest giving to. You, of self.

Ho, but the switch of selfhood
    rides a bulging team:
mountainous mind and pitching will and volcanic heart and quaking tissues
— runaways, forging and forming and wrestling with
their fallen chevalier,
    this scarlet lucifer who hides in my branches
and laughs at us with his high white teeth and onyx eyes
and tells us the tale of all the world, his bright brain cocked
and his beguiling face, and the golden apple he holds in his hand
looks good, and we aspire to its polish and its art, it is the abstraction of all
the virtues we aspire to, we burn to acquire to, to excel to, and
proudly
        we burn
            in hell
                can I pray
    to be still
    and to wait
    and to look
    and to listen
    and to see clearly
    and to take my punishment without flinching

what is peace what is war but the life in our soul?

    Look in the sea, and the wet face of your childhood will be
borne out, moon soul.
Water catches light, purples and clears. Color lies
    a radiance
upon the sea, washes out like dye, respires
in the throws of the
tide, the recoils: jockeys
the pale horse from Apollo's stable to the deadly
night shade. Rainbows a London bridge for the
child-heart.
        Pieces
of eight, the sun
      recovers.
We hold, like grapes,
by the frailest ladder,
our maturity: catch, with our breath, the next new hint

in the air of the tenderest next step on the ineffable hair
    of the strip we must walk if we dare, the tenderest trip
        from adulthood to child,
    the bell in the breast open and clear and
  the softening flesh, stouthearted and lined with the acts
that have labored and born, ring through our lives from birth to death
  the quest for the child that rises like dawn like leaven like milk
    in the bosom that feeds, and we suck on this teat and the
      platitudes fade,
    the spirit peels its garments away and
  stands unconcealed, who is it, who is this person, where do we point,
at what hour do we stand in the
flood and the fire, the burning sand, the kingdom of heaven is now
at hand, the now and forever, you cannot repeal the law of the light,
you cannot withstand the animate hand, you are born and you live
and all beings rejoice
        in your perpetual anniversary,
                        drops of glory
like honey exudes from a bee, drops of love, body's wine, sweet
nectar of union, the fair light heart of the noblest knight
of the realm and his lady, the fairest too, and their child
    we do recover,
  all love's children bide and be.

        Blessings, athlete
              who trounces in the mask of Eros.
        Blessings, savior
              who launders the trudging soul
          Lips
              that press the forward push of breath
         Voyager
              mobile and intact, continuously
              shedding oneself like old skin,
              the bud of oneself continuously
              pushing out, of one's own darkness:

O light's the bunch that clusters there
we tend our fate on a pliant stair
stand supple in the trials of air

We bring to sweetness that child's grace
prepare a place for that true face
fire and flood is that true face

hovering grace in all our human pain.

     The child who wept and who weeps
still
     I take in my arms for its tears are alive
and carry life out my eyes, down my cheeks, down the cracks of the earth
for the yield.

        Keep the waters flowing, Aquarius.
Indwell, Crab. Fertilize, Goat. Inhabit, Fish.
Voyage, Ram. Gore, Bull. Hunt, Lioness. Bear, Virgin, and preside, O
Queen. Weigh, Scales. Embrace, Twins. Be your own self,
Scorpion. Take aim, Archer, and shoot

   a fierce shaft in the quickened blood
   to unite, to unite,
   to enjoy.

        The child
within
     freshens in
         the shadows.
Dreams hang in
       festive galleries;
imagination turns to deeds the force
that shaped
      our size.
The eye be blank till the stream within
  carry us to our
periphery, and we stand, not eyes,
   but souls,
      beholding
what the spirit beholds. Beings be lit
in the ten thousand things.
    Plastic artist,

fashioning oneself and one's temple, child,
a racer,
    wades like a holy seer
into the draughts one drinks,
    entranced, swallows the shimmering view.
    Swells
like bellows the divine exchange,
    a cosmic breathing
between ourselves and all the worlds which we
    inhale.

In the big face of flesh, sits, a sleeping Buddha,
    the child, flashing.
With these beams, blinds
    the organ eye.
    Finds
        the way on.

Block Island, July 3, 1959
Stony Point, August-September 20, 1960

The Light this Late Day Casts

I sought for Love in the woods
where I had seen Him last

where in my trembling vision
He had awakened and fled

and now, in discouragement and grief,
I returned to search the place

drawn by a sense of infusion in the air
of that measureless union

pressed by a heart that swelled toward the pools
and hillsides of His visit.

To all the features of that space
I saw His face bequeathed: measuring
the atmosphere with summer's rapture
from within.

. . . sweeps His smile through the woods,
dashes light, the trickle of jet to the bright bomb,
mineral kings crowned colors of trees,
jade, agate, topaz, carnelian,
suspended cities, boardwalks, bridges,
mosaics and steppingstones dripped and flung,
visionary pueblos, flowering temples and pits,
a Presence
curls and floats and expires;
breathes through His pipe
warm music for life's slumbering oracles. Quick,
to the quick points the electric touch.

Truly, the farther into the woods I went,
the farther up the stream I climbed,
the more deeply I returned into His aura,
the more cleansed and naked . . . —

the more His pulse and ardor built
until in the chaste and voluptuous brake
I fainted dead away, and fell,
a dead leaf in His invisible arms.

His Being humped in the stream:
He was a dragon frothing and dragging the stones,
and the stones ground their teeth in blessedness.

His brown transparent watery body
flowed and humped and rattled the stones,
and the aroma of the stream smote me anew.

I sat on a granite island and assumed His shape;
sloped over the rock, and the back of my legs an arch
of His trouble, my toes tracing themselves in Him
and He leapt up and batted miraculous crystals.

I walked tenderly at the edge of the stream
and my tears fell with yearning into the body of Love
and they disappeared, and appeared again between the lashes of the spray.

I searched everywhere with my soul and my gaze,
and I lifted my eyes over the earth nearby.
On a rock at the base of a bank, a handful of gold —
limp and almost drained of its matter — and I suffered anew.

The summer is dying, the autumn is clear,
the autumn is dying, the winter is in flakes,
fast into the heart of the earth where the sun descends
runs the river, the loaves of its brown body rise
in the light this late day casts.

O *the Bonny Cheer of an Ancient Day*

O the bonny cheer of an ancient day
bacon-bright and coffee-thoughtful,
I love its dawn and the dawn in me
of my neighbor's child, when she comes lolloping
down to her school-life and waiting soul,
when I marry her!
Today has its nose in her tattering hair;
I'm pulled by the hand, we hug and we eat
and somehow the last love of our lives
breaks fast here.

Poems from The Crossing Point
1973

Three Wisdoms

"Go slow," said the snail.
"Hop! Hop!" said the hare.
"Pace yourself," said the cheetah, "it's a long run."

Holy Poems: Prayers

Prayer One

All that I hate and am
against
be exorcised. Be spent
as day is; was.
Gladly to do, I hereby
stamp and spit thrice and
mew in
      spite. All
gone, I want it to be
all gone. And everyone's
           as well.
Calumnia, all hail! farewell!
I'll practice dying every night,
breathe first each A.M. and
no more turn aside to brood on
fate or scope or sum.
Creator spirit, be with me now
as unattended I
persist.

Prayer Two

Litchfield
      loony-bin
holds me dear. I
swear, wall-eyes
can hear. Make it so,
make it so — I would be
near to thee, crazed boy
and girl, be near to
vandal life and limb.
Strike my heart dumb to
falsify, seal my lips sweet
to kiss.
Creator spirit, be with me now
to down the draught
of ill.

Prayer Three

I would give a million bucks
    to be free of the past.
Another million, to levitate.
Three, to get going.
Double the bet, to be nowhere and
    love it.
Giving odds on all practices
    perfect and imperfect.
I would sell out to the species,
    to space, to
the sport of it.
Creator spirit, my money's down.

Prayer Four

Put some sense into my head, lord,
and I'll get after it.
Fallow, my hello lies for your ring.
Tattle, lord, on the void's high halo
and hunch is, I'll be tuned; and
timed to the split. Cut through, father,
my blood runs in circles. And
Wichita's my state. All plums I'll heap
and cattails piled in feathers, all
sticky buns and pornographic pleasures I'll
be sure. Lord, take my hand and place it
on the prick of thou that I may
sow and hallow.

Prayer Five

Magnify thy works, lord, and I'll
be seeing you: wherever the salsify roots
and the ground's ground underfoot.
Tenderfeet, shut eye, will follow thy gleam
as big as life and twice as visible. Oh why not,
why not pick the pocket of tares and
holly thorns — red berries of blood
that never runs cold, red summer's
treat, blind with the
splendid brand. Magnify those works of
yourn and my squint will stare
well, to the loveless
ever-leafing void. Of hope and the five
wants. Hoarfrost, Indian pipes, and greenswards.
For heaven's sake, god o'th'heart,
who thou art, to be at quits with.

Runes

Rune 1

4 hens
4 black hens
dance.
Il pleut. It
is raining and weeping.
Ses pieds grattent.
See how the legs tremble and
   paw
backwards
the straw.
How the neck trembles
   and turns
the feathers and flesh
   alive
in the dance.
Come. Come.

Rune 2

How the little bird sings
out of himself
his song.
How long
   it takes me to find him
he is so small in the tree
   so singing in his dance.

Rune 3

how the catkins tremble
      with their shape
         so soft
      in the air
like wattles
      in a dance
the soft combs of hens
      the soft bird

how they dance
        in winter
        to the spring—

How they dance
        in winter
        to the spring within them
the springing up
        the source and waters,
        well.
Hear it scratching the ground
hear it mounting the tree
see it changing the color
                of twigs.

Rune 4

JADE RABBIT
Yoko Ono told me
        in London
I was born in the year
of The Dragon,
conceived in the year
of The Rabbit.
She said
it is hard
for a woman
to have been born in the year of
The Dragon.
Jade Rabbit,
born to fire,
conceives
in terror and screams.

Rune 5

Hyde Park, February 5, 1967
LOOK:
The maple trees in Hyde Park
are sending tiny fireballs flying
out the ends of twigs

yet holding by a thread
as Juliet dreamed of holding Romeo,
and sending sparks, tiny, bright at the tips,
a dusk of spring's first aura
thickens in this afternoon.
I look into the lane of crowns
and suddenly light darkens into life,
surfaces of trees flame molten red.
Awakening brims at the verge of sight.
Somewhere overhead some bird is racketing
a dozen voices and as many songs,
what kind of creature steaming so?
I catch him with my eye, a catbird;
and across the space a fat ring-necked dove
purrs and shifts her weight.

Rune 6

I wake after long sleep
to catkins, snowdrops, daffodils.
The night within
turns to day, and yet
the nightness of its knowing
flows within the light.
On waking
I may no more separate my night from day
but feel them breathing
inward and outward.
On waking now
I may not leave the night behind
but see it grow in the ovary
as the snowdrop wilts —
night darkens the white petals,
swells in the seed.
On waking
I stand in the door.

Dream, Pentecost

The dark red hollow of my mouth:
a room, a black tenebrous room, a hellish tryst, the dead
of night, infernal aura burning within the walls,
drapes sinks rugs tables chairs curtains
and toward each other we step, my teacher and I,
into the center of this distance:

I am in a dark chamber with my teacher
who is short and Semitic and in tweeds and his hair is dark and curly
and close to his head, his nose is arched and in the grottoes of his eyes
flash golden fires, his face is all acurl with flame
and force and smiles, and life-lines folding into flesh,
and the ruddy dark look of his blackness and his gloom
and the fiery essence of his dark power and the wreaths
of his wrinkling features fathomless where they start,

I am in a dark chamber with my beloved teacher as never before.
He kisses me full upon my mouth
a full kiss that has no passion in it,
and in between my lips his absolute black tongue passes
like the deft head of a snake lifted by muscle
slipping and stealing dark and purposefully
between my lips.

                    I was astounded. The dark
chamber, my teacher, my lips, the dark gliding
penetration of the tongue, the contact —
a picture and a sensation and a portent
I cannot be rid of.

        What speech presses he into me?
        What illumination gestates behind those walls?

        The gliding mind and the womb of the throat,
        the stealthy assured pressure, knowledge
        enters the dark cave where self is rooted in the bite of the teeth,
        is spread through the skull in branching aisles. The clean
        unpsychological unpassional entrance of my teacher's
        speech into my mouth portends. By Lucifer's light
        knowledge finds its orifice,
        the female organ awaits by destiny the tongue

114

that speaks in it.
All parables of love and genesis:
the word sounds
                    down the forming scale
and spirit flutters up from the ground.

Homage

Sun-up /
over the valley's lip a running glaze,
lake, crazed and curdled.

Sun-down / and
the dense rim fires
nut-black, bone-brown.

Stoneware is the night,
its granite foot, aside, the hills,
trimmed sills and shallows. O bene,
bene,
blessed be the jars that
burn with day, turn smack
center on the whirring dark.

For Karen Karnes: Clay Has a Way

Clay
has a way, of making seed streets for vagrant birds,
soup saddles to hold us thirsty riders,
clay corned to a bitter red
and straddled and thinned down to blue,
I say, clay
has a way of being plastic
and without residue, we sing
to the one who works it so.
We sing: soul, and shaper.

      This is a birthday.
      This is Karen, devoted to the plainspeaking of clay
and its parables.
      This is our pleasure,
           To listen to her vessels' cuneiform,
           To respond with a verse
           and to love the speaking dust.

Concerts of Space

for Lucy Rie

I was looking at a friend's bookshelf
                    this morning
and I thought I saw a book with the title:
                    "CONCERTS OF SPACE"
and my heart leapt!: "What a poetic title!" I exclaimed,
        (hearing music of the spheres and heavenly harmonies)
and then my gaze lengthened, and the words read:
        "CONCEPTS" OF SPACE. Never mind, I said to myself,
                                (and perhaps aloud),
I shall write a poem and call it "Concerts of Space,"
and it shall be for Lucy Rie
        and the cup and saucer she made, and gave to me on Sunday.

Your pots are decisions, Lucy Rie,
        decisions, forms, and emblems: *mots*.
No, no, they are pots of clay,
timbres of darkness and light,
suffered through, come safely through.
Your hands, Lucy Rie, conduct them through the fire:
                                "concerts of space."

Archangel Michael

This first turned tree, a maple,
stands absolute for iron:
green of spring, red of autumn,
marry in deep fathoms' fire.

I see its face in surfaces of leaves,
in roots, in earth that feeds them,
in water, air, and sun. The face:
Dear Michael of the Autumn Colors,
Dear serious face, dear sword of consciousness,
with your flaming lance dance us awake!

We rouse from summer sleep at the tomb's edge,
this second Easter: this fall,
from foliage into color, from color into spirit,
from spirit into humankind.

Our wintry resurrection already is preparing
in these flags of leaves, its Festival of Color,
inward turning. Invisible to sight, new hues
are visible, risen light!

Oh Micha-el, your mighty countenance
quickens us into withering,
quickens the seed forth,
marries tomb and fountain
in mysteries of earth.

Oh Micha-el, in your countenance we trace
our new heart,
our new face.

An Art of Fire

perfects
     the mystery,
completes
     the life-line of
     our common clay.

Potters transform
     like alchemists of old
     crude earth into *le pierre qui vive*
     FIRE   IN   THE   STONE

They shape their kilns to tongues of flame,
     its food and rule,
pacing the flow of fuel, the hold of heat,
the cooling,
alert to tame the elemental blaze
                         into life-vessel for
                         Aquarian Souls.
Self-creation is an art of fire:
                         each person
                         forms
                         our spirit's housing
                         and
                         celestial cistern.

Poems from Toward Wholeness

1980

Chief Crazy Horse at Fountain Hall

I like it here: big teepee
       big directions: sun rise set
              north star south
              big axis
              world cross
              four winds
      big colors in small pieces
        my horse crazy with mana light
      me big chief, crazy fountain.

I like
   crosses: two dark on dawn-down-under leaves' light,
      window spirits,
      in kiva crypt.
         Stepping stones of sun jewels
           for souls at their rain source,
      in planetary round dance.

        Corn sun king god
      comes pale yellow and green
        in middle window
      sweet eyes lightening from afar.

I like
   these green horizons.
                    Light
                in the cup
           and the center a lamb,
            a spilling fountain,
          blood in the earth red a
             crazy mystery,
             big chief mystery.
       Crosses black like empty night:
               eclipse:
            dark spirit doors:
          a whale, a scorpion.

    This
    cup
       running over

crazy with truthful giving
   and
the highest window of red sounds
   and blue horses of light.
My horse runs in your spilling windows,
   o crazy fountaineer.

I like it here: your hall,
   big teepee,
 big heaven door cross on ceiling for spirit eyes
 on floor earth cross for spirit calling dance.

These signs: good medicine.

 I chief Crazy Horse of Indianos
breathe in my breath
     the speech of your temple.
     Good medicine
will sing now its way
    welcome in our land.

Vigil

for Sister Marita

In this leveling laughter of time
    guess what stone crib crumbles,
guess who waits to bloom, who brings kisses and crumbs,
guess what befalls, as fall we do here before this cave,
    this place of fire
        in stone
        in grace
this intimate cold light bright chamber
of every-which-way life and love, this past-all-knowing touch.

Thirsting to wait, blind, empty, a primal ear,
carrying something I do not know, my hands are full.

    O recollection, this bayberry day
    O sacred play, O jewel of joy, O let me wait in this blessed cold.

Ethereal arms of snow fall like music in crystal scales
from brows of angels curving like geese on the wind . . .
O sister . . .

    Waker of day, behold in this grail stone manger your bread and blood.
    Behold us swimmers reach your rock, your dove-perch lovers' bed.
    Canticle: O ring!

Wait oh let me wait here, to hear, in the silence of waters:
    "There is but one altar," you said, "one prayer."
Let me see speaking the sea-spoken dayspring everywhere,
    your white stone and morning star!

    Let it be barren, this light. Let it be no light.
        Let it be bedrock: and absolute birth.

Poems from
The Public School and the
Education of the Whole Person

1980

Opening Anthem

We do not scold the cock for calling dawn,
the cow for lowing when her day is done:
a time for rising, a time for bedding down,
a time for travelling to the town and home again.

Life has her seasons, teaches us her tides.
Says, "Wait! Reflect!" Says "Leap! Give all!"
We follow in her wake in little boats
getting the feel of currents as we ride.
We put to sea or seek the shore with equal joy.
We climb the mast or set the grate below.

Our song is deep within us for the work:
to keep the faith, to worship and to grow.
The Vine winds through us, spring and fall:
now lush in fruit, now wizened bough.

Wholeness we bear within us like a seed:
to die, to grow, to sleep and grow again.
It is the mystery of person and of world,
of inner fire and flavor and respect.
It is our name, our home, our neighborhood.
We are its art. It forming makes us good.

The schooling that we seek is full within.
It rises to the surface as we move.
It has the face of angels, human speech.
All present borderlines are lit with warmth
like autumn maples tilting in the sun.

Our planet is our school, and far beyond:
our church, our shop and study, and our fields.
We are all learning to awake:
awake in dream, in meditation and in prayer.
Inspired awake! Inspirited awake!
We feel it thus: one mighty school, the teaching everywhere.

Closing Hymn

Sweetness stores in the root,
sap rises and descends.
The rhythms of our nature
round us round.

Human Beings, risen,
take eternal life in hand.
Our creative light
shares in world creation.
The Life-Line of our Schooling
is its golden vein.

Christmas Poems

1951 - 1980

Christmas Sonnet

Love clapped His hands He surely did and laughed
To feel the breast, the soft blue wool, to drink
In milky streams that run from heart to lips,
To wake and feel his form a man's. I think
The cow and the ass both lowed and brayed,
And the magi bowed, and the shepherds prayed
And the angels sang. And the birds flew in
And out the eaves, looking sideways at Love
And blinking, and jumped into space and swam.
And carillons played and the saints gave in
And the world was rocking with magic waves
That spill at our feet. O my love, my love ...
This time of our year he is ours to bear,
The infant God, and we are his heirs.

Christmas Song

Every year
on Christmas morn
we all sing out
a child is born!

What does it mean?
As certain as space
as certain as time
this birth takes place.

Mary on fire
from a holy dove
bears a child
whose father is love.

A cosmic spring
from groundless ground
to earth from heaven
the sun turns round.

In depthless dark
life-seed is sown
invisible man
fire in the stone.

Certain as death
certain as grace
certain as doubt
new birth takes place

again again
solstice, spring,
summer, autumn
and Christmas king.

Little by little,
steadily sure,
in seasons' wisdom
our lives mature.

Little by little
freed of the past
our future reaches
his arms to us.

Holy baby
every year
you seek us out
by coming near.

How cunning is
your secret art
of feeding the fire
that shapes our heart,

how speechless
the word in your infant face:
THIS REALM IS
EACH ONE'S REALM
IN EACH ONE'S PLACE.

Wherever we are
you choose that place.

Wherever we are
on Christmas morn
you choose that manger
to be born.

How secret and sure
your living pulse
bears us inward and
onward thus.

You are born
yet you bear us.

Mary bears you
and you bear us
what mysterious vintage
sun-infused!

An art of fire,
New Being is born
in earth and cosmos
on Christmas morn!

The Winged Seed

for Olive Whicher, co-author of
The Plant Between Sun and Earth

Sing, oh muse,
 the winged seed,
 borne to earth
 in loving deed.

Manger its soil,
 stable its field,
 love-filled chalice
 our seedling's yield.

Sing
 cow and ass
Sing
 shepherd and sheep,
Sing
 star and angels
the babe asleep.

Come
 root and shoot
Come
 core and crown
 ROSE IN THE SEED
 BEARING THE SUN.

Sing, oh heart,
 NATIVITY!
Thy Christ-child's birth,
and births to be —
 the winged seed's
 geometry.

O Christmas Babe of Seed and Birth

Baby Jesus, I see your breath flutter the fins of a paper fish
        telling a new wind . . .

        You are swaddled in tasseled tides
        and bounced in emerald laps across horizons.
        You play with light
        and your tiny feet twinkle in the night sky.
        Your hands are made of clay. Already they
        sow the seeds of transformation.
        Faithful little farmer, every year you cast in us
        fresh grain and wash the soil, redeem the air
        and pacify the poisoning fires.
        We spread our knees to your coming;
        the mouth grows wide in wonder
        as you seek the world through us.

Baby Jesus, your pulse beats in my body
        as I breathe the new wind.
        I hear you cry:
        "Be kind. Be merciful. Forgive.
        Have courage for distress. Be brave
        toward ills more grievous than your own.
        Play in the night sky! Blow the paper fish!"

This mystery of birth is in our flesh.
        We kneel to the furrow,
        place the kernel, model our caring,
        handle the coals. Christed,
        earth bears its healing cup.

Baby Jesus, I feel you at dawn exhale the sun,
        I hear you slap the breakers and call up the day,
        I see your ancient infant heart distilled
        in prophecy. "I am new ground," you sing:
        "Sow me, reap me, feed on me, die in me."

O Christmas Babe of Seed and Birth,
        inspiring wind that blows us forth,
        plant deep the rhythms of our growth.

Christmas 1980: Love Is Not a Ready-made

Beloved, the dazzling blue and turquoise waves
of your body pulse to the horizon.
Stiff-legged birds embroider your shore.
Your heart swells and moves beyond sight.
Your hands are the grace of my longing.

But so much suffering, Beloved —
your skin ulcerous and torn,
your organs cancerous and strange.

Such disasters — killing —
homeless hordes — so much pain,
so many tears — such wretchedness.

Out of these bits we make the nest?
the cradle? for our child, Beloved?
human hope and divine forgiveness?
courage to press on?

The Christmas Babe rejoins us
faithfully. A pulse of love
beats in the stench of sickness and ill will.
Greed sings its carols, rings its bell.
Pride pats its belly, laughs Ho! Ho!
The plugged-in donkey brays,
the plastic infant wails, the wise men turn mechanically around.
In all this falsity, human feelings drown.

Beloved, at this moment, in despair,
I look into my heart and find you there,
intact, where you must be,
in life, through thick and thin.

You touch me with your blue, your green,
your birds, their dance, your wasteland
and disease. Through all this worldly horror,
your pure speech weaves:

"Love is not a ready made.

It is an impulse of the will,
a Christmastide of sowing seed,
of sowing birth, of sowing new.

"This seed may ripen into growth.
In time new human hearts
may learn to give themselves away.
In time the earth may be the Christmas star."

I hear your voice, your call
to learn to suffer and to heal,
to quicken love in inner will.

Beloved, wake in me your truth,
creative art of Christmas birth.

A Christmas Poem for My Sister

On opposite sides of the North American continent we dwell,
each by an ocean: you by the great mother of sleep, and I
by the lashing quickener of life and legend. Oceans we lie
along: you on your couch, leaning toward death; I sprawled
and striding, hand over my eyes, against the fire.

I listen to the sea murmur her secrets and feel your presence
here, in me, you too hearing the moods of her song,
your fingers lazy on the strings of our ocean.

As long as I've known you, death has been your secret lover.
"I'll die at 39" you said when we were children. "Enough - not 40!"
The love you dreamed of would come, you said,
when you died and all your friends would mourn —
and the love would crest, would flood, an ocean you could drown in.
For 30 years you begged your body for release —
threatened to die before our eyes - imagined yourself gone.
Somehow you never took this life in hand, not really,
never had the stomach for it, though you shine so vital, bright and glossy —
as if more deeply betrothed, like Persephone,
to the Lord of the Shades, the Son of the Waters.

Our lives dig deep their channel,
shape their last transcendent birth canal.
We are squeezed toward these waves, happy, and
choosing the slip where our keel unfastens. O my sister,
I have dreaded your dying, until just now, here, east,
the sun floats up pink and yellow from under the sea —
the moon slides blue, out and up, the sky.

Somehow this Christmastide (this swing
of birth and sun and moon and starlight,
this manger deep who rocks the suffering seed)
opens the strange and secret portal.
The door you wait to enter
breathes light.

I see the ripples lapping at your baby feet,
your cradle swaying as the wavecrests break.

I hear you laughing to be you again.
The Self Who Loves You
wakes beneath the tree,
the Death you love
smiles in the dawn.
Angels fly between your brows
and you ride the waves and sing.

Truly, sister, Christmas is a floodtide beyond dream.
Love crests in Life anew,
beats in the bright dark
before and after.
Now gathered as a Yuletide wreath
its wavelets twine upon your door.

Poems for
Paintings by Thomas S. Buechner, Sr.

1986 - 1988

"White Daffodil"

The painter unfolds his easel
and the shadows change color. He
lifts his palette into the light.
One bud fills with green.
It goes to white as petals form.
The painter guides the leaf to its apogee, its curve and point.
Light licks the bract into rose-red.
Light stains yellow as white fades into it.
The trumpet of the flower
sounds a long vowel: "I know you at last."
      The painter pauses, the flower leaps
across.

"Survivor"

How shall a barn speak of its heat and stench,
the fullness of its granary — oh
wild fields uplifted!

Now its walls bend in the ground. The
foundation calls out, "I am here."
Embedded in azure, the tints of sky,
the survivor grows like crystals, —
in edges, planes, and thrust of the peaked roofs.

We stand, looking, in a purpling green;
move forward into dimming russets and creams:
a field begins to lighten
in the gradually encircling sun.

The painter catches with his brush
the whispered breath of an elder —
this Being whose definition does not die.
Wind whipped, bleached, bitten by time,
it shines on this hill. Oh
radiance surviving! Oh
mother of stables in the burnish of age!

"Lemons"

The lemon, the $1/2$ lemon, the slice,
the table top, the wall, shadows,
the bright sheen of the peel,
the waxy surface.

Before ever I loved the painter,
I loved the painting.

The primal THING,
color, taste, touch,
aroma; movements of cutting, squeezing,
rinsing: the timeless fruit
of time lived,

not the color
of budding willows, banana, orange,
nor yet of grapefruit. Lemons: at once
richer and more distilled than the taste
of fresh grass.

The power of the small, the celebration
of sacred space and of what fills it:
Mandala window with white center
and rays to the periphery.

O lemon, it is thou! —
in the begging bowl reflected,
in the brushstroke the goldfinch
the salmon berry
the invisible painter holding the twig.

"Luke"

Childman, in your theater of color
disguised — a moment before you speak
… standing in daisies up to your waist,
white with dark centers … a troubled sky …
something pink and fallen from
the firmament, collage of rose and purpleblack.
Behind a dirge of indigo maroon,
dawn flickers.
The painter selects his brush of light
and opens the curtain:
> standing against a field of flowers/
> colors falling and rising/
> sun through a window, the rose/

Is it you, Luke, in the numinous
blue of your shirt (your sheath)
and the sanguine darting flares of spirit
drawn from your redgold hair, mouth, nose
and shadow down your neck? The brass
belt buckle, something torn on your sleeve?
Green lustre at the horizon billows up
into peach blossom and redviolet. Your shining face
is bright with flesh.

"Homestead": Easter

Beyond the shadowed trailer, a white streak,
the sun's path,
splits the canvas left to right.
A wedge of silence
calls us to the edge of time.
　　　　Inside, the painter sleeps.
He waits for darkness to thicken, to
become the light he sees by.
　　　　Outside, the antic branches of trees,
the unresponsive chill of frozen fields:
a lottery bought with nightmares
of rebirthing.
　　　　Awake, over the white vein,
over the snowy foreground, a golden wash
begins to settle
into the color of life-before-life:
a greengoldenlavendergrey, sculpting
the rough terrain. Plump forms of clouds
or hills squat above the scene.
Through them a sunrise aura mutely
surges.
　　　　In this homestead plays
the painter's irony: that such a
faceless housing should be home!
Yet may be home!
No door nor threshold visible, no
person calls — that just here
should be the play of opposites
we celebrate in the heart's core:
loss, absence, the Good Friday rape
of hope, and silent Saturday, waiting
for the Easter sun.
We play it out, this drama
of dying to old riches,
breath rising new — weak
though we may find ourselves
at the equinox of spring.
　　　　Dark in the wintry trees,
subtly this homestead takes on gold:
trembling icon at the edge
opens the tomb, softly oh softly
to intimate birth.

"Barn Frame, Big Flats"

All the weight is overturned,
slips away, leaves
like a carapace the barn shell,
further eaten away
as the sea will,
the wasting peril of time
consuming.
　　　The painter listens for
transparency. He guides us through
the boarded walls, through roof and hay mow.
Intervals (the space between) open, and
the mass of barn transforms into
geometry: a drawing,
of right angles, tri-angles, struts,
perpendicular veins softly rigid
of decaying wood. Colors of mountains and
of sunset glance off remaining beams.
　　　And in the lap of the frame
the greens of wild growth,
patches of amber - and through the empty doorspace,
an opaque blue of distance:
grey with heat, yellow with dawning.
　　　The painter is witness to birth
everywhere that the light changes,
new seasons in the grass and
on the hills, where fragility endures
and death blooms invisibly.
　　　Here is a long fidelity
to this garden, watching the
timbers fall, one by one, the holes spread,
till in the moment of painting,
the painter mirrors the lasting
in what does not last.

Nude: "Red Afro"

Her hair fizzes into a dazzling, de-
monic thicket. The painter has flooded it
with carmine, indigo, siena, ochre,
a froth of supernatural passion
waiting to condense (or perhaps
never to condense) — we imagine ourselves submerging
in that seductive halo, finding
another world where we swim unencumbered
with desire, another dimension united
as divine lust — the god for the
maiden, for the youth, Psyche for
Eros. Is this the wicked boy's doing as well?
The frizz of electric arrows, a mane
which is a bull's eye, smitten.
    It's the militant nipples, swollen
and pointing, that arouse my eye
each time I turn to this painter's images:
sensual, exciting, dangerous in combination with
the hidden Pan-like mask of the face: the
splotches of red, unhealthy looking, entranced . . .
below the wild wig of a femme fatale, bouffant . . .
        Why do I stare as if you might
at any moment
                    awaken, shift position, reveal more?
        Wild woman, sister, take me into your
glance. Through your eyes (unfocussed, somnolent)
let me see the painter painting.
He stops at the rib cage, just above your navel.
The lower torso one can only imagine — perhaps
of a magical animal, like a female centaur,
or a mermaid half-fish.
            The body of this nude — dare I call her
"woman," she seems more than that!
Fire weaves a fine net through her skin.
Strawberry birthmarks look scraped
and enflamed, eyes half closed by their heat.
The gold ring in her left ear seems girlish
in that environment of hair, shoulder, nipple and all.

157

Listen, red Afro, I am here waiting in the wings.
The painter does not go below your waist.
Dissolved in lust and pleasure, we
take thy body as a cup, drink it, and lose consciousness.
Aha, so that's who it is! MEDUSA!
and all your coiling and uncoiling snakes,
and serpentine aura, the excruciating hair!
Ecstatic we summon the forces of stone,
eager to die in the breasts of Medusa ...

How have you defeated us, Oh painter sub-
lime? How have you made the distance pure
between us, uncorrupted ... compassionate ...
forever vulnerable?